Key Issues in Education and Social Justice

Education studies: Key issues

In the last fifteen years or so Education Studies has developed rapidly as a distinctive subject in its own right. Beginning initially at undergraduate level, this expansion is now also taking place at masters level and is characterised by an increasingly analytical approach to the study of education. As education studies programmes have developed there has emerged a number of discrete study areas that require indepth texts to support student learning.

'*Introduction to Education Studies*, Second Edition' is the core text in this series and gives students an important grounding in the study of education. It provides an overview of the subject and introduces the reader to fundamental theories and debates in the field. The series, 'Key Issues in Education Studies,' has evolved from this core text and, using the same critical approach, each volume outlines a significant area of study within the education studies field. All of the books have been written by experts in their area and provide the detail and depth required by students as they progress further in the subject.

Taken as a whole, this series provides a comprehensive set of texts for the student of education. While of particular value to students of Education Studies, the series will also be instructive for those studying related areas such as Childhood Studies and Special Needs, as well as being of interest to students on initial teacher training courses and practitioners working in education.

We hope that this series provides you, the reader, with plentiful opportunities to explore further this exciting and significant area of study and we wish you well in your endeavours.

Steve Bartlett and Diana Burton

Education Studies: Key Issues Series

Steve Bartlett and Diana Burton: *Introduction to Education Studies,* Second Edition (2007)

Stephen Ward and Christine Eden: *Key Issues in Education Policy* (2009)

Diana Burton and Steve Bartlett: *Key Issues for Education Researchers* (2009)

Alan Hodkinson and Philip Vickerman: *Key Issues in Special Educational Needs and Inclusion* (2009)

Key Issues in Education and Social Justice

Emma Smith

Los Angeles | London | New Delhi
Singapore | Washington DC

KH

First published 2012

SAGE Publications Ltd
1 Oliver's Yard
55 City Road
London EC1Y 1SP

SAGE Publications Inc.
2455 Teller Road
Thousand Oaks, California 91320

SAGE Publications India Pvt Ltd
B 1/I 1 Mohan Cooperative Industrial Area
Mathura Road
New Delhi 110 044

SAGE Publications Asia-Pacific Pte Ltd
3 Church Street
#10-04 Samsung Hub
Singapore 049483

Library of Congress Control Number: 2011930552

British Library Cataloguing in Publication data

A catalogue record for this book is available from the British Library

ISBN 978-1-84920-810-9
ISBN 978-1-84920-811-6 (pbk)

Typeset by C&M Digitals (P) Ltd, Chennai, India
Printed in Great Britain by CPI Group (UK) Ltd, Croydon, CRO 4YY
Printed on paper from sustainable resources

MIX
Paper from
responsible sources
FSC
www.fsc.org   FSC® C013604

5/1/13

Contents

Author biography

Emma is Professor of Education Equity and Policy at the University of Birmingham. She has previously held posts at the University of York and at Cardiff University and also as a Chemistry teacher and SENCO in the South Wales valleys. She is interested in equity issues in the field of education and in the role that educational policy can play in reducing inequalities and closing achievement gaps. Recent research has focused on boys' underachievement, barriers to participation in Higher Education, pupils' views of fairness and equity in school, teacher education and the impact of the *No Child Left Behind Act* in the USA.

List of abbreviations

AACPA	André Agassi College Preparatory Academy
AYP	Adequate Yearly Progress (Nevada, US)
BIS	Department for Business, Innovation and Skills
CELS	Citizenship Educational Longitudinal Study
DCSF	Department for Children, Schools and Families
DEFRA	Department for Environment, Food and Rural Affairs
DES	Department of Education and Science
DfE	Department for Education
DfES	Department for Education and Skills
EHRC	Equality and Human Rights Commission
EMA	Education Maintenance Allowance
FSM	free school meals
GCSE	General Certificate in Secondary Education
GDP	gross domestic product
HE	higher education
HEFCE	Higher Education Funding Council for England
HESA	Higher Education Statistics Agency
ICT	information and communication technologies
IEA	International Association for the Evaluation of Educational Achievement
ILO	International Labour Organisation
LSN	Learning and Skills Network
MP	Member of Parliament
NAEP	National Assessment of Educational Progress (US)
NAO	National Audit Office
NCEE	National Center on Education and the Economy (US)
NCES	National Center for Education Statistics (US)
NCIHE	National Committee of Inquiry into Higher Education
NCLB	'No Child Left Behind' (US)
NEET	not in employment, education and training
NESS	National Evaluation of Sure Start
NFER	National Foundation for Educational Research
OECD	Organisation for Economic Cooperation and Development
OHCHR	Office of the UN High Commissioner for Human Rights
ONS	Office for National Statistics
PCAS	Polytechnics Central Admissions Service
PIRLS	Progress in International Reading and Literacy Study

PISA	Programme for International Student Assessment
SEAL	Social and Emotional Aspects of Learning
SES	socioeconomic status
SSLP	Sure Start Local Programme
STEM	Science, Technology, Engineering and Mathematics
TIMSS	Trends in International Maths and Science Study
UCAS	Universities Central Admissions Service
UCCA	Universities Central Council on Admissions
UKCES	UK Commission for Employability and Skills
UNCRC	UN Convention on the Rights of the Child
UNESCO	United Nations Educational, Scientific and Cultural Organisation
UNICEF	United Nations Children's Fund

Preface

This book is about fairness and social justice in education. While I was writing it during the summer of 2010, it was striking that I really did not have to look very far before coming across the word 'fairness'. Following a general election in which the three main political parties used the word extensively and where two even used it as part of their election slogans, 'fairness', it appears, is in fashion. The BBC has been running a series of programmes to explain to us what fairness and justice are all about. And when the widely anticipated Equalities and Human Rights Commission Report was published in October 2010, we had the answer. Fairness, we were told, was 'as British as fish and chips'.

But beyond the whiny remarks of a child (*it's not fair*) or its legal use to mean the right to a fair trial, what does fairness really mean? Our Prime Minster has told us that fairness means giving people what they deserve, although what they deserve does depend on how they behave (Cameron 2010a). The Equalities Review published in 2007 also told us a great deal about fairness and equality. An equal society is one that

> protects and promotes equal, real freedom and substantive opportunity to live in the ways people value and would choose, so that everyone can flourish. An equal society recognises people's different needs, situations and goals and removes the barriers that limit what people can do and can be. (p. 109)

Fairness it seems is also the right to be different.

Perhaps it should come as no surprise then that fairness is a difficult term to define and measure. It can mean different things to different people. For instance, we might favour fairness in treating everyone equally (equality of opportunity). Or we might decide that fairness is treating people differently so that certain outcomes can become more equal and, therefore, more fair (equality of outcome). Take an example from the field of education. We might argue that it is fair that all schools are funded equally. This might make the opportunities for those who attend them fairer, regardless of where they come from. But would we argue that is it also fair for teachers to treat all pupils in the same way when they are in the classroom? Consider the child with literacy difficulties or the child who is a gifted writer. Would it be fair for the teacher to treat them the same all of the time? Is it fair as well for teachers to discriminate between pupils by punishing a pupil who misbehaves, or rewarding a pupil who has shown talent or effort? Depending on our answers to these questions we may decide that we want equality in some things but not in others.

This book provides an introduction to issues of fairness, inequality and social justice in education. It draws upon aspects of research, policy and contemporary thinking in the field to provide a guide to the educational inequalities that may exist and persist throughout an individual's educational trajectory. The book considers the educational experience as lifelong and takes a look at the inequalities that may accompany us from birth, throughout our schooling and into the formal and informal modes of learning that we may decide to undertake later in life.

The first chapter will introduce some of the key conceptual and policy perspectives on issues of inequality and social justice. Then, before beginning our focus on educational inequalities, Chapter 2 will take a broader look at the nature of inequalities in wider society with particular attention to inequalities in areas such as health, housing, employment and early years provision. Chapters 3 to 5 look at educational inequalities as they apply to schools and the pupils that attend them. They examine the extent to which the ideal of good-quality schools for all children is evident today. We look at whether education policies over the last 30 years have raised standards, closed achievement gaps and ensured a more equitable school system for all. We consider, in particular, inequalities in the attainment of young people from different racial, social and gender groups, as well as in the inclusion of children and young people with special educational needs.

In the current educational climate, examination success is frequently seen as the most tangible outcome of schooling, but what of the role of schools in producing socially and morally responsible citizens? Chapter 6 will look at the area of pupil voice and the views that young people hold on whether they feel that their teachers and schools treat them fairly. Chapters 7 and 8 continue our interest in educational trajectories and take a look at post-compulsory education and training. More people in this country have access to higher education than at any time in our history. But is this the sign of a more equitable educational system? Chapter 7 will look at the expansion of the higher education system in the context of the widening participation agenda and review the extent to which different social groups may have benefitted. In Chapter 8 we consider those who do not go to university and the choices and opportunities that are available for them. Chapter 9 is the final chapter which draws together the key ideas that were introduced in the book and asks how, and whether, any inequalities might be overcome.

As you can see from the outline here, the topic of education and social justice is vast. There is much that we cannot cover in this book. We do not have the space, for example, to look at issues of global justice and inequality. This is certainly not because the experiences of young women in Afghanistan or efforts to ensure universal primary education in sub-Saharan Africa are of no concern to us. It is simply that in a book of this nature we cannot include everything. Therefore the book takes a very Anglo-centric view of social justice and inequality. Its examples are drawn mainly from the UK, with some small reference given to other developed nations, notably the United States. The theoretical perspectives that the book presents are similarly limited when compared to the extensive coverage the area usually receives in other educational textbooks, and the book is like this mainly for that reason. Similarly, as social justice is a key political issue it would be remiss not to draw heavily on contemporary political views and ideologies. This means that a great deal of reference is made to political and sociological issues, arguably at the expense of the psychological and cultural.

The area of education and social justice is large and changing. To assist students to keep up to date with topics and because there was much I could not fit into this book, I have developed a website to accompany the text. Here I have provided links to additional reading and videos which will hopefully help you explore the topic in much more detail. The website can be found at www.educationandsocialjustice.co.uk.

Writing this book has been an interesting and largely enjoyable experience and I would like to thank Christopher Robertson, Ian Davison, Jim Middleton, Ryan Mowat and Stephen Gorard for their helpful suggestions and advice. I would particularly like to thank Patrick White without whose patient willingness to talk through my ideas this book would have taken a lot longer to complete and have been a lot more difficult to do. He is an excellent and thoughtful critic and I am very grateful to him.

I would like to dedicate this book to the Maisies. To my grandmother, Maisie Matthews, who left school at 14 to look for work in Merthyr Tydfil during the Great Depression. And to my new baby niece, Maisie Smith, as she takes her first steps to playschool just a few miles up the road from her great-grandmother's home. Her parents are so proud and full of optimism – her grandparents have been instructed to start saving for university. Their experiences of our education system will inevitably be different. How different remains to be seen.

A fair society is an open society, one in which every individual is free to succeed.

No one should be prevented from fulfilling their potential by the circumstances of their birth. What ought to count is how hard you work and the skills and talents you possess, not the school you went to or the jobs your parents did.

(*Opening Doors, Breaking Barriers: A Strategy for Social Mobility*, Cabinet Office, May 2011)

1

An introduction to education and social justice

Education is the greatest liberator mankind has ever known and the greatest force for social progress.

(Gordon Brown, speech to the University of Greenwich, October 2007)

The role of education in promoting equality and social justice is a major preoccupation of the politicians who play a central role in deciding what is taught in our schools, where it is taught, to whom and by whom. From James Callaghan's speech at Ruskin College, Oxford in 1976 to the current Coalition government's commitment to education as the engine of social mobility and economic growth, the purpose of schooling has become increasingly linked to politicians' views of what constitutes a fair and just society. This chapter introduces some of these politicised views of education and social justice and their impact on what we understand by a fair and equitable school system. This chapter examines what we mean by social justice. It focuses on three basic principles of justice: fairness as defined by treating individuals according to merit, by treating them according to need and by treating everyone equally. The final section brings together these ideas in order to compare different perspectives on the purpose of education in contemporary society.

The Politics of Social Justice

Over the last 30 or so years, different political ideologies have given rise to different notions of how the state should promote social justice through education. The policies that schools experience today, such as the National Curriculum, school choice, high-stakes testing and school accountability through league tables, have been the result of different political views on how best to achieve a world-class education system. The role that education can play in promoting social justice has been particularly prominent, with parties on both the political Left and Right seeing education as key to reducing social inequality:

> Without good education there can be no social justice. (Cameron 2007: 84)

> It is education which provides the rungs on the ladder of social mobility. (Brown 2010)

As the above quotations illustrate, the role of education in reducing inequality and promoting social mobility is a favourite topic among politicians seeking to share their vision for a fair and just society. However, while politicians from various parties may agree that education has a key role in promoting social justice, they differ in their views on the best way to achieve it. In this chapter we will examine these different political ideologies by focusing on extracts from the speeches of recent and current British political figures. To begin, let us consider this from the former Prime Minister Gordon Brown:

> ... fairness can be advanced by but cannot, in the end, be guaranteed by charities, however benevolent, by markets, however dynamic, or by individuals, however well meaning, but guaranteed only by enabling government. (Brown 2005)

Gordon Brown's view is that while charities, individual effort and markets can work to make society become fairer; the main responsibility lies with the government. His argument that 'only the State can guarantee fairness' sits in contrast to that of the current Prime Minster David Cameron. Cameron's view is of a 'Big Society' where power and control are redistributed from the state to individuals and local communities – in other words, a movement 'from state action to social action' (Cameron 2009). In essence, this is the reverse of Gordon Brown's view. For the new UK Coalition government, limiting the role of the state in educational matters is exemplified by plans to expand the academy schools programme and the establishment of new Swedish-style free schools (both of which are examined more closely in Chapter 3). These initiatives will mean a lessening of the control that government and local authorities have over how schools are administered. In the case of academies this will involve allowing the most 'outstanding' schools increased autonomy over the curriculum, admissions policies as well as teachers' pay and conditions. For critics who consider the role of the state to be crucial in ensuring educational equity, such proposals are tantamount to privatisation (for example, Bousted 2010; Ball 2007).

Brown and Cameron's views about the role of the state in enabling social justice reflect fundamental differences in the ideologies of the Conservative and Labour political traditions. Traditionally and put simply, the view of political parties whose ideologies lie to the Left (i.e. Labour) is that the state has an important role to play in ensuring that people's life experiences are fair. Political parties whose ideologies lie further to the Right (i.e. Conservative) argue that individual rights and responsibilities, rather than the state, are paramount. A fuller discussion of the historical and philosophical roots of these ideologies is beyond the scope of this book but Box 1.1 provides an example of how these political perspectives relate to issues of poverty and education.

Box 1.1 Summary of political viewpoints on the relationship between poverty and education

The view from the Left is that the inferior educational experiences of the poor hold them back and prevent them from competing with better educated groups. Therefore the poor are forced into low-waged and menial work and social mobility is stalled.

The view from the Right is that the poor are poor because they failed to work hard and take advantage of educational opportunities. It is their individual responsibility to take hold of the opportunities that are available and so prosper.

The moderate view is that the poor are poor because of inadequate education partly because of inferior schools but also because of disrupted families, for example, which prevents them from absorbing the education that is available.

(Thurow 1977)

A good illustration of how the two main political parties differ with regard to the role of the state and the individual can be seen by examining the views of two recent long-serving Prime Ministers: Tony Blair (1997–2007) and Margaret Thatcher (1979–90). One of the most famous recent examples of a leading political figure challenging the role of the state in ensuring social justice was Margaret Thatcher's 1987 interview to *Woman's Own* Magazine (Thatcher 1987). In what is known as the '*Society Speech*', Thatcher argued that rather than relying on the assistance of the state, people should assume responsibility for their own lives:

> I think we have gone through a period when too many children and people have been given to understand 'I have a problem, it is the Government's job to cope with it!' ... 'I am homeless, the Government must house me!' and so they are casting their problems on society and who is society? There is no such thing! There are individual men and women and there are families and no government can do anything except through people and people look to themselves first ... *There is no such thing as society*. There is a living tapestry of men and women and people and the beauty of that tapestry and the quality of our lives will depend upon how much each of us is prepared to take responsibility for ourselves and each of us prepared to turn round and help by our own efforts those who are unfortunate. (Thatcher 1987, emphasis added)

Thatcher's view of the primacy of individual rights over collective rights (Thatcher 1985) extends to her conception of 'social justice', a term she considered to be unclear and imprecise and which corresponded to a 'doctrine' that was being promoted by a 'progressive consensus' whose view it was that the state should be responsible for promoting equality (Thatcher 1975). Thatcher's own views were somewhat different. Consider this from a speech she gave to the Institute of Socioeconomic Studies in New York:

> ... the pursuit of equality itself is a mirage. What's more desirable and more practicable than the pursuit of equality is the pursuit of equality of opportunity. And opportunity means nothing unless it includes the right to be unequal and the freedom to be different. One of the reasons that we value individuals is not because they're all the same, but because they're all different. I believe you have a saying in the Middle West: 'Don't cut down the tall poppies. Let them rather grow tall.' I would say, let our children grow tall and some taller than others if they have the ability in them to do so. (Thatcher 1975)

Margaret Thatcher was quite clear in her view of the diminished role that the state should play in ensuring equality and social (or educational) justice. She emphasised individual rather than state responsibility and while promoting a concept of 'equality of opportunity' also defended an individual's right to be different and, by extension, unequal.

Tony Blair's New Labour, on the other hand, was far less sceptical about the term 'social justice' and explicitly linked it to education:

> To those who say, 'Where is Labour's passion for social justice?' I say education is social justice. Education is liberty. Education is opportunity. Education is the key not just to how we as individuals succeed and prosper, but to the future of this country. (Blair 1997; see also Pyke 1997)

In his pamphlet *The Third Way*, which was published towards the start of his premiership, Tony Blair (1998) argued forcibly for a politics that moved away from 'Old Left' ideals of state control and away from a 'New Right' that treated social issues 'as evils to be undone' (p. 1). While it is quite difficult to define what the Third Way actually means (Dale 2000), in Blair's view Third Way politics advocate an 'enabling' government that, passionate in its commitment to social justice, would harness the power of the markets to serve the public interest (p. 7). The Third Way sees social justice and equality as resting on four values: equal worth, opportunity for all, responsibility and community (p. 3).

In the thirteen years that Labour was last in office, issues of social justice underpinned most of their social and educational policies (Hills and Stewart 2005; Hills et al. 2009). Their record on social justice and the extent to which they have succeeded in making society fairer is explored briefly in Chapter 2 and in much more detail in two edited collections by John Hills and colleagues (Hills and Stewart 2005; Hills et al. 2009). But it is clear that improving social justice and social mobility were explicit aims of the two most recent Labour governments, as Blair's successor Gordon Brown reiterated:

> So instead of, as in the past, developing only some of the potential of some of the people, our mission for liberty for all and fairness to all summons us to develop all of the potential of all the people. (Brown 2005)

In May 2010, David Cameron became the leader of the first Coalition government the country had seen since the Second World War. With office came Cameron's idea for solving the problems of what he calls, 'Broken Britain'. His view of a 'Big Society' presents its own conceptualisation of justice and equality:

> Of course in a free society, some people will be richer than others. Of course if we make opportunity more equal, some will do better than others. But there's a massive difference between a system that allows fair reward for talent, effort and enterprise and a system that keeps millions of people at the bottom locked out of the success enjoyed by the mainstream … Instead, we should focus on the causes of poverty as well as the symptoms because that is the best way to reduce it in the long term. And we should focus on *closing the gap between the bottom and the middle*, not because that is the easy thing to do, but because focusing on those who do not have the chance of a good life is the most important thing to do. (Cameron 2009, emphasis added)

For Cameron, the 'Big Society' represents the empowerment of ordinary people to take charge of their lives through strengthening communities and civil society. This might involve enabling parents to start their own schools (see Chapter 3) or encouraging people to undertake more voluntary work or charitable giving. Either way it involves 'taking power away from politicians and giving it to people' and, so Cameron argues, enabling society to become fairer (Cameron 2010b).

Here we have seen different perspectives on the role of the state in ensuring social justice: Thatcherism viewed justice as the primary responsibility of the individual rather than the state and upheld an individual's right 'to be unequal and the freedom to be different'. In contrast Tony Blair and Gordon Brown, in particular, advocated a far greater role for the state in ensuring social justice. Then there is Cameron's idea of fairness as giving people what they deserve: a 'fair reward for talent and effort' and of 'closing the gap between the bottom and the middle' (not, you will note, between the bottom and the top). Despite these different political views of the extent to which the state should or should not enable social justice, the notion of a fair society is central to contemporary political policy. Therefore an understanding of social justice, and by implication of educational justice, is crucial in order to appreciate the ways in which education and schooling might work to reduce society's inequalities. It is to these different principles of social justice that we now turn.

What do We Mean by Social Justice?

So far in this chapter, we have read about how politicians conceive of 'social justice' and 'fairness' as central to reducing inequalities and making society fairer. But how do we decide what is fair and what is unfair?

Before considering how educational inequalities manifest themselves and the extent to which schools can reduce these inequalities and promote educational justice, it is worth pausing to consider what it is that we mean by social justice and equality in the first place. This is not necessarily straightforward and is an issue that has preoccupied philosophers since the time of Aristotle and Plato. What follows is a very basic introduction – further reading and resources are given at the end of the chapter.

Consider the following definition of justice:

> Justice is the constant and perpetual will to render to each his due. (Miller, quoting Roman Emperor Justinian, 2003: 76)

This notion of treating others according to what they are due or entitled to implies that people have different needs and therefore ought to be treated differently. So the hungry or the sick ought to be given more resources than those who are healthy or better off. Sometimes this can be straightforward. Often, however, it is not and the problem we have is in deciding who deserves what.

Miller (2003) and Garner et al. (2009) provide us with three concepts to help us decide this:

- First, the way we treat people has to be *consistent*, so if students behave in similar ways then any punishments or rewards have to be applied in the same way.
- Secondly, this treatment has to be *relevant*, so we might not reward or punish an individual because their name begins with a certain letter of the alphabet, for example.
- Finally, it has to be *proportionate*, so if we have to treat people differently that treatment ought to be in proportion to what they have done, so you might not reward someone with a thousand pounds for handing in a good end-of-term essay.

While these concepts may guide us in how to treat individuals in ways that they deserve, they do not tell us when or under what circumstances we are justified in doing this, what it is that people are owed or due, nor the grounds on which we are justified in treating them differently. Such decisions are subjective and of course depend very much on the context in which they take place. Thus they require different values and judgements about what is the 'right' or fair thing to do (Sandel 2010).

So the key issue at stake here is one of entitlement or giving people what they are due. But how do we decide this? Take the following example:

> Pete and Sam were both given a piece of homework by their teacher that needed to be completed by the following day. Pete went home and spent the evening researching his homework using the Internet and writing his findings up neatly, and submitted his work the next morning. Sam also completed his work on time but he scribbled it down quickly on the school bus that morning. When the marks came back Pete received a Grade A and Sam a Grade D.

Most people reading this scenario would probably argue that it is fair that Pete received a higher mark than Sam. Pete put a great deal of effort into his work – whereas Sam did not – and that effort ought to be rewarded. But what if we then found out that Sam's home life was very difficult. He had to care for his sick mother and look after his younger siblings. He had no access to the Internet at home and was not able to visit his local library because he spent the evening cooking for the family and caring for the younger children. Knowledge of Sam's circumstances might perhaps make us think differently about how he was treated.

The complexity of deciding what is fair and unfair and developing principles to guide us in making this decision has preoccupied philosophers for centuries. However, in our everyday lives we frequently have to make decisions about actions that might be fair or unfair. For example when deciding which type of school to send our children to, or being asked to listen to politicians' views on how they wish to apply the principles of social justice to improve society.

As you can see from the example of Pete and Sam, when we consider issues of justice or fairness they tend to be about distributing particular rewards or punishments to individuals or to different groups of people. This type of justice is called *distributive justice* and asks us to think about the ways in which we distribute the benefits of society, such as wealth, income, educational opportunities and other resources. There are different ways in which we might do this.

We might, for example, decide to reward everyone *equally* and decide that no one ought to be treated differently and that everyone should get the same resources. Or we might decide to distribute resources according to *need*. So, in the example above, Sam is arguably in the most need of support due to his complicated family life, so more resources should be given to him. However, Pete worked hard and achieved a good mark and therefore he deserves to be rewarded based on his *merit;* after all that was the purpose of the assignment. This is another way to think about how we allocate our resources – according to *merit or desert.*

So we have three principles to help us think how we might treat people fairly:

1. People should be treated according to their merit or what they deserve.
2. People should be treated according to what they need.
3. Everyone should be treated equally and in the same way.

What Principles Might We Use to Understand What is Fair?

These ideas of rewarding an individual based on equality, need or merit are key to understanding the different principles of justice. We will consider them in more detail below.

Ruitenberg and Vokey (2010) conceptualise these three principles in the following ways:

- *Justice as harmony* – based on principles of merit or desert.
- *Justice as equity* – based on principles of need.
- *Justice as equality* – based on principles of equal treatment.

Justice as Harmony

We start with Plato's conception of what Ruitenberg and Vokey (2010) call *justice as harmony*. This approach argues that people have different talents and that these different talents, when put together, will strengthen the community as well as society more widely. Education should seek to support these different talents and by doing so will help enable individuals to reach their (different) potentials. We can see this principle in use throughout the education system in the UK: in the post-Second World War tripartite system of grammar and secondary modern schools; in the division of vocational and academic qualifications and in contemporary programmes to encourage school diversification.

The following example should help us understand this more clearly:

> Sarah is an excellent swimmer. She arrives at the pool each morning at 6 a.m and trains for two hours before going to school. On the basis of her swimming success, Sarah wins a scholarship to a highly prestigious school.

According to the principle of *justice as harmony* Sarah should be rewarded for her hard work and commitment and should consider winning this scholarship to be a just reward for all her effort: in other words, she *deserves* it. A contrary view, however, is that justice based on merit or desert, in this case, is unfair. Sarah's success is based – at least partly – on her natural talent and she doesn't deserve the rewards this should bring. Other students may work just as hard as Sarah – perhaps in even more challenging circumstances – but because they are not endowed with a natural talent, they have no way of profiting from the benefits of that talent in the same way that Sarah does. For some, this may be a fairly contentious view to take. Sandel discusses this issue in more detail at www.justiceharvard.org/.

But first consider the same argument from a slightly different perspective:

> Susannah attends the same school as Sarah. However, Susannah comes from a wealthy family whose parents can easily afford to pay the large tuition fees. Susannah is not especially talented, nor does she particularly enjoy school, but because she was born to a wealthy family she is able to enjoy the benefits of an excellent education.

Would we raise the same objections to this situation as we might do to Sarah's case above? Perhaps not. Your opinion might depend on your views of private education and perhaps your own experiences of school. One might argue, for example, that Susannah is lucky that she was born to a wealthy family; this privilege, unlike that of Sarah, was not borne out of hard work and so she simply does not deserve to receive such an education. In other words, this scenario might be considered to be more unfair than Sarah's because Susannah's reward (an excellent education) is based on neither merit nor talent. However, an opponent of this view of justice might strongly object and argue that it is Susannah's parents' right to chose the best education for their daughter and that it is unfair and an affront to their liberties to prevent them from doing so. I am not going to try to resolve this issue here but hopefully you can start to see some of the difficulties of applying different principles of social justice. Interestingly, this view that Susannah's parents should have absolute freedom to choose the education they think best for their daughter resonates with a Libertarian view of justice which holds individual freedom of choice as paramount. There is an excellent introduction to Libertarian views of justice in Sandel (2010).

Leaving the issue of private education to one side for a moment (it is something we return to in Chapter 3), let us consider another principle of justice.

Justice as Equity

A somewhat different principle of justice is one of *justice as equity*, possibly the most well-known proponent of which is John Rawls (see Box 1.2). Rawls argues for an egalitarian notion of justice, the key aim of which is to reduce inequalities. To understand how Rawls' notion of justice might be applied to education, consider the following vignette:

> Jacinta has difficulty reading and finds it hard to keep up in class. The teacher has to spend a lot of time helping Jacinta and gives her a lot of attention. Sometimes the other students have to wait for the teacher to stop helping Jacinta and to come and help them.

Our response to the fairness of such a situation might be:

- that Jacinta needs extra help so it is fair that the teacher should spend more time helping her;

or:

- that the teacher should spend equal time with all the students. It is not fair that others should have to wait.

A supporter of the *justice as equity* argument would say that the first option is the fairer, in other words that it is justifiable for the teacher to treat the students differently in order that their opportunities for success become more equal. Jacinta needs more help and she should therefore receive it in order to give herself the best chance of success. The basis for this argument is that not all students are the same. Instead, they are different in terms of what they need in order to be able to reach a particular level of achievement (Brighouse and Swift 2008). This might be because they come from a disadvantaged social environment, have special educational needs or speak a different language to the one used in school. This would mean that in order for them to achieve similar educational outcomes to more advantaged students more resources would need to be given to them.

Box 1.2 Rawls' theory of justice

John Rawls (1921–2002) was an American philosopher who is credited with producing one of the most influential works on political theory of the twentieth century. Rawls argues for a liberal egalitarian view of justice, two principles of which are:

- Each person has the same indefeasible claim to a fully adequate scheme of equal basic liberties, which scheme is compatible with the same scheme of liberties for all.
- Social and economic inequalities are to satisfy two conditions: first, they are to be attached to offices and positions open to all under conditions of fair equality of opportunity; and second, they are to be to the greatest benefit of the least-advantaged members of society.

(Rawls, 2001: 42–3)

Thus Rawls holds basic liberties as paramount (such as access to a basic education); only when these basic rights are assured is the second principle relevant. This second principle is interesting because it enables inequalities to exist within society, as long as first everyone has an equal chance of securing these advantaged positions (through equality of opportunity) and that these inequalities serve to benefit the most vulnerable in society. Thus it is acceptable for individuals to earn large amounts of money, provided that part of that money is redistributed to the least wealthy through the taxation system.

According to Rawls inequalities (in terms of attainment, income and so on) are justifiable only when they benefit all of society, including the least advantaged. So, for example, it takes many years to become a doctor and when they are finally qualified they tend to work long, often unsociable, hours. Therefore it is fair that doctors earn more money than window cleaners, for example, as their work is of far more benefit to society (particularly its least advantaged members – in this case the sick). It is also acceptable for doctors to receive more education and training than window cleaners as this enables them to fulfil their job to the benefit of everyone. However, Rawls is also quite clear that the different treatment that doctors receive, in terms of the amount of money they earn and the education they receive, is only justified if everyone is able to benefit from better medical care. He also argues that all individuals should have an equal chance of gaining the advantages that being a doctor confers. So, for example, everyone should be able to have access to the education which will lead to the qualifications that would enable one to take up this role – so the opportunity for anyone to train to become a doctor has to be present.

Given that around 60 per cent of medical students in the UK come from 'middle-class' backgrounds (the average for all undergraduates is 36 per cent) (Smith and White 2011), one might ask whether the 'benefits' of being a doctor are actually being shared by everyone and whether in this instance, Rawls' principles of justice are being met.

> ## Further reading
>
> There is an excellent introduction to Rawls' work in Michael Sandel's book: *Justice: What's the Right Thing to Do?* (2010).

Justice as Equality

Both *justice as harmony* and *justice as equity* advocate treating people differently. However, with *justice as harmony* different (and possibly unequal) outcomes are expected; the hard-working student deserves more help from the teacher and it is likely that this will be reflected in higher test scores. With *justice as equity* the intention is to equalise an individual's opportunity in order to facilitate more equal (and arguably fairer) outcomes. Here the less able student receives more help from the teacher in order to bring their test scores up to a similar level to their peers.

One further principle of justice – *justice as equality* – takes a slightly different approach. This argues that although people are not the same, they are equally deserving, so equal treatment is essential even if the eventual outcomes are themselves unequal. This would favour the second option in the extract above: Jacinta's teacher ought to devote the same amount of attention to all her students, even if this means that some students will achieve lower grades.

The idea that students should all be treated in the same way is widely held. It is the principle by which UNESCO's Education for All programme requires that all children are entitled to free, accessible primary-level education. It is also the principle under which the comprehensive system of schooling that we have in most parts of the UK operates, as well as being the standard by which many school children decide whether or not they have been treated fairly by their teachers:

> [Teacher] listens to the opinions of pupils who have good marks, but he ignores others who have low marks or who he does not like. This is strange. Teachers should not differentiate pupils. (Japanese student, in Gorard and Smith 2010)

> In history, the teacher's 'favourites' don't get punished, can walk round the room, even walk out of the room, and not get punished. The rest of the class isn't acknowledged. (English student, in Gorard and Smith 2010)

However, there are powerful arguments against the principle of equality of opportunity: central for most people is the belief that people are different and should therefore not be treated in the same way, either because they *deserve* or *need* to be treated differently. Another view is that treating everyone the same will simply lead to mediocrity where the best will not be able to excel and the 'weakest' will struggle, or as Edward Burke (1790) famously wrote: 'Those who attempt to level never equalise.'

Table 1.1   Summary of the different principles of justice

Principle of justice	Type of treatment	Type of outcome
Justice as harmony	Different	Different
Justice as equity	Different	Similar
Justice as equality	Similar	Different

In this section we have introduced three basic principles of justice. They will be returned to throughout the book and are summarised, in terms of their relationship between how people are treated and the outcome of this treatment, in Table 1.1.

As you will hopefully have seen from the above examples, coming up with one clear definition of justice is very difficult and these three principles of justice are complex and often contested. Which one you favour might differ according to your political ideology or the context in which you seek to apply them. So, for example, a free-market libertarian, a welfare liberal and a socialist are likely to have very different notions of justice, each of which fit perfectly logically into their own ideological perspectives. It is also likely that we would apply different principles of justice in different situations. So we might argue that examination grades should reward merit, resources allocated to students with special educational needs should reflect need and equality should dictate mandating free primary education. Indeed, as Miller (2003) argues, it is the context in which the (in)justice takes place which is crucial. According to Campbell (2010) there may be no one 'correct' way of looking at justice; instead there might be several different interpretations, all equally valid. In fact it 'may be a mistake to have an overall theory of justice which has an equal force in all spheres' (p. 9). That different principles of justice may apply in different situations certainly makes understanding and conceptualising educational justice challenging. But it also makes the study of this topic interesting.

In this section we have introduced some of the complexities surrounding the idea of justice and three key principles that can help us to decide whether something is fair or not. We have also read about how education, and schools in particular, are considered to be key agents of social justice, especially in the minds of contemporary politicians. But how are schools able to fulfil this important function? Is it realistic to expect schools to have such a profound impact on the life chances of the students they educate? In the next section we look at three different perspectives on the function of schools.

What are Schools for?

The public understands the primary importance of education as the foundation for a satisfying life, an enlightened and civil society, a strong economy, and a secure Nation. (NCEE 1983)

Whatever their differing ideologies on how best to achieve a more just society, the political consensus that education is at the heart of social justice issues does give rise to the question: what are schools for? In this short section we will introduce three potential functions of schooling: the role of schools in producing a highly skilled workforce who will help ensure the economic productivity of the nation; the philosophers' view of the holistic role of schooling; and finally an alternative perspective on the apparent harm that our current education system brings to those that we seek to educate and care for.

For many policy-makers the answer to the question 'what are schools for?' would seem to be that they are there to prepare the next generation of workers and that 'education is the best economic policy' (Brown 2007). This view, however, is not uncontroversial. In her excellent book *Does Education Matter?* Alison Wolf suggests that 'our preoccupation with education as an engine of growth has … narrowed – dismally and progressively – our vision of education itself' (2000: 254). She argues that while an overwhelming case can be made for the state's involvement in basic education, the millions of pounds that are invested in generating a 'knowledge economy' – through the expansion of the post-compulsory education and training sector – has simply resulted in expansion as an end in itself. According to Wolf the consequences of expanding provision for education and training, in particular through the rapid increase in university places, have done little to benefit the most vulnerable in society – those for whom the general education system has failed. Such a view is particularly pertinent in light of the government's current plans to raise the school leaving age to 18 from 2015. These are important issues for those interested in educational justice and it is a theme to which we return in Chapter 8.

The wider purpose of schooling, beyond the purely economic, has preoccupied philosophers for centuries; indeed, it is a topic that is as 'old as philosophy itself'. That major philosophers from John Locke to Leo Tolstoy to Bertrand Russell have concerned themselves with the topic is evident from the numerous books which share the title 'On Education' (see, for example, Brighouse 2006). Unsurprisingly there are many different views on the nature and purpose of education and schooling and interested readers would do well to begin with the edited collection of papers in Bailey et al. (2010).

However, one widely held view among contemporary philosophers of education is that 'the central purpose of education is to promote human flourishing' (Brighouse 2006: 42). In advancing his perspective Brighouse argues that schools 'should orient themselves to the needs of the children who will have to deal with the economy, and not to the needs of the economy itself' (2006: 28). He goes on to suggest four functions of schooling, which should enable children to:

- become 'autonomous, self governing adults' (p. 131);
- become economically self-reliant;

- 'lead flourishing lives' (p. 42);
- become 'responsible, deliberative citizens who are capable of accepting the demands of justice and abiding by the norm of reciprocity' (p. 131).

The view that education has a key role in encouraging children to flourish places greater emphasis on the role of schools in helping shape the next generation of 'socially and morally responsible citizens' than is currently apparent in our education system. It is a view of education that is at odds with the current preoccupation with academic standards, and suggests a notion of schooling that is closer to Pring's (2010) conception of an educated 19-year-old who

> ... has a sufficient grasp of those ideas and principles to enable him or her to manage life intelligently, who has the competence and skills to tackle practical tasks including those required for employment, who has a sense of community and the disposition to make a contribution to it, who is morally serious in the sense that he or she cares about fairness and responsibility to others, who is inspired by what has been done by others and who has a sense and knowledge of self-confidence and resilience in the face of difficulty ... Such an aim should shape the education for the future. (p. 63)

The role of schools as mini communities or societies is something that we return to in Chapter 6 when we explore the opportunities that schools and the curriculum provides students to develop and flourish as active, engaged citizens. Next, however, we consider an arguably more negative aspect of schooling that is at odds with our general conceptions of schools as fair and caring places.

In his book *Toxic Schooling: How Schools Became Worse*, Clive Harber (2009) takes issue with the widely held assumption that enrolment in formal schooling is a 'good thing', arguing instead that schools serve to perpetuate and reproduce inequalities. In addition:

> ... schools far from consistently and uniformly being institutions of care and protection in fact both reproduce and cause violence. Not only do they not necessarily protect pupils from different forms of violence in the wider society, but they actively perpetuate violence on pupils themselves. (p. 4)

Harber presents synopses of a number of key texts written during the 1960s and 1980s (including the book by Illich (1971) on deschooling) that examine the extent to which children's experiences of school deviate from the idealised role of schools as agents of social reform. The book makes difficult reading, with schooling variously characterised as oppressive, dominative, indoctrinating, deferential, docile, institutionalised, taming and controlling. Harber argues that dissatisfaction and unease with schooling is not new; neither has it lessened in the decades since the books he covers were written. While the educational ideologies followed in schools such as Summerhill (see Box 1.3) might provide a counter to much of what Harber argues is wrong with our current school system, they are not without controversy and arguably sit uneasily with many people's notions of what an effective school might be.

Box 1.3 Summerhill: an exercise in democratic schooling

Summerhill is an example of a progressive school whose philosophy, according to its founder A.S. Neill, is to 'make the school to fit the child, instead of the child to fit the school' (Neill 1964: 4). Founded in 1921 and located in a village in Suffolk, England, Summerhill is an independent school teaching around 80 children aged 5–17. It is a school which has made famous the notion that children should be free to decide for themselves how to spend their time: there is no compulsory timetable, exams only for those who wish to take them and no adherence to particular teaching methods. It is a place where everyone, from the head teacher to the youngest pupil, is treated equally and with respect, and where rules are made and changed with the consensus of the entire school community (Neill 1964). Since its founding, Summerhill has drawn much criticism: Max Rafferty, a former Superintendent of Public Instruction for California, described the school as a 'dirty joke' which 'degrades learning to the status of a disorganised orgy' (Rafferty 1970: 24). Possibly the biggest challenge came in 1999 when the school inspectorate, Ofsted, criticised the school for an 'abrogation of educational responsibility and a failure of management and leadership' (Ofsted 1999: para. 11); it further concluded that 'the instruction is not efficient or suitable' (para. 29). Happier times have returned following a successful Ofsted inspection in 2007 that, in acknowledging the school's particular philosophy, praised as 'outstanding' the spiritual, moral, social and cultural development of Summerhill pupils (Ofsted 2007).

Further reading

Neil, A. S. (1964) *Summerhill: A Radical Approach to Education*. London: Victor Gollancz.
Vaughan, M. (ed.) (2006) *Summerhill and A. S. Neil*. Buckingham: Open University Press.

There is a list of recommended reading on the school's website: http://www.summerhillschool.co.uk

Summary

This chapter has provided a brief introduction to some key topics in the field of social justice and how they might apply to education. We have looked at a few of the different philosophical perspectives on justice and seen how politicians apply the term both to education and to society more widely. The chapter concluded with a brief overview of some perspectives on the different functions of schooling: both positive and negative. However, whatever one's view about the most appropriate way of ensuring that educational opportunities are as fair as possible, it is nevertheless the case that there are many diverse ways in which inequalities can and do manifest themselves within schools. For example, some pupils achieve better examination results than others, attend more 'effective' schools or have longer school careers – thus educational opportunities and outcomes are not distributed equally. It is useful to remember that it is those pupils who are the least academically successful who tend to have the shortest school careers and who may end up leaving school without even the most basic skills. This is not to argue that those who aspire to a career as a lawyer should not have longer educational careers than those who aspire to less 'skilled' jobs, but it is worth reflecting upon how we, as a society, choose to allocate our educational resources. It is also important to consider that remedying society's injustices is not simply the responsibility of teachers and other educators. As we shall see in the next chapter, unfairness extends far beyond the school gates.

 Reflection

Consider the following extract from a Year 9 student's report of fair treatment in school. Which different principles of justice might you apply to decide whether or not their experience of school is a fair one?

The boys deserve the punishment they are given (and the girls too) because when they mess around they disturb hard-working pupils. But the punishment doesn't work. Most pupils have no respect for anyone in the school. The better pupils should be placed in a separate class so they can work undisturbed and get the most out of school. (Female student, in Smith and Gorard 2006)

Additional Resources

Below are a number of resources on issues of social justice. None of these sites focus explicitly on issues of educational justice but do provide a very useful introduction to wider concepts of justice and fairness. Michael Sandel's Harvard lectures are particularly good.

Michael Sandel's 'Justice' lectures

Michael Sandel's Justice course is one of the most popular in Harvard University's history. The website provides televised access to Sandel's 12 lectures, as well as discussion guides and suggestions for further reading. It is an excellent introduction to the field. You can access the lecture on http://www.justiceharvard.org/.

Open University resources on justice

In parallel with the BBC Justice season, the Open University hosts a useful website on a number of topics related to social justice. Resources include downloadable

MP3 files exploring topics such as blame and historical injustices, justice and the law, and moral aspects of injustice. It also provides access to study units that provide a basic introduction to political philosophy: http://www.open.ac.uk/openlearn/whats-on/ou-on-the-bbc-justice-season.

The history of education in England

Education in England is a very useful web-based resource that provides historical information on the development of education policy in England. It provides a chronology of important events plus access to the full text of many important government reports and papers, including the full text of the 1967 Plowden report on primary schools and the 1963 Robbins report on higher education. Access to the site is through http://www.educationengland.org.uk/index.html.

Further reading

Brighouse, H. (2006) *On Education*. Abingdon: Routledge.

Harber, C. (2009) *Toxic Schooling: How Schools Became Worse*. Nottingham: Educational Heretics Press.

Miller, D. (2003) *Political Philosophy: A Very Short Introduction*. Oxford: Oxford University Press.

Sandel, M. J. (2010) *Justice: What's the Right Thing to Do?* London: Penguin.

Wolf, A. (2000) *Does Education Matter? Myths About Education and Economic Growth*. London: Penguin.

2

Social justice and inequality

Never will I believe that what makes a population stronger, and healthier, and wiser, and better, can ultimately make it poorer.

(Thomas Babington Macaulay, House of Commons, 22 May 1846)

Before sharpening our focus on educational inequalities, we will first take a broader perspective on the nature of inequalities in wider society. This chapter looks at inequalities in areas such as health, housing, employment and income and concentratess on inequalities between the poorest and the wealthiest groups in society. We start by looking at the extent to which material poverty is an issue for individuals in the UK today before considering how being poor is related to health and other social inequalities. We will then look briefly at how income inequalities in the UK compare with those in other developed nations. Poverty and inequality do not just affect adults and so the final section of this chapter will consider the impact that growing up in poverty has on the lives and early educational experiences of young children.

Income Inequalities

Britain is a wealthy country. It is the world's sixth largest economy in terms of gross domestic product (GDP) (OECD 2010a), and in 2008 the median (middle) gross weekly income for an individual in full-time employment was £448 (National Equality Panel 2010). Modern Britain is not a country we associate with poverty or with the pictures of starvation, deprivation and desperation that are beamed to our television screens from distant parts of the world. Neither is it a country where people 'survive' on less than a dollar a day (the widely used definition of absolute poverty). Yet it is nevertheless a country where the differences in wealth between the richest and the poorest have been described as 'shocking' (BBC 2010a, National Equality Panel 2010: 2). According to a recent report:

> Britain is an unequal country, more so than many other industrial countries and more so than a generation ago. This is manifest in many ways – most obviously in the gap between those who are well off and those who are less well off. (National Equality Panel 2010: 1)

Poverty is a difficult term to define and measure. Even the poorest families in Britain are wealthier than many who live in the world's developing nations and far wealthier than they would have been had they lived one hundred years ago. However, poverty is a real factor in the daily lives of millions of people in the UK. But poverty is not just about having little money, it is also about not having access to the things that the average citizen takes for granted – from owning material goods such as a computer to being able to afford a holiday. Additionally, the consequences of being poor – poor health and poor employment prospects – can also work to deny an individual the opportunity to play a full part in society. While there is no universally agreed definition of poverty (Korkodilos 2007) the European Union adopts the following working definition:

> The poor are those whose resources (material, cultural and social) are so limited as to exclude them from the minimum acceptable way of life in the Member States in which they live.

This measure of poverty, which considers how well off you are in comparison to those who live around you, has led to many researchers defining poverty in relative terms: usually as whether or not one lives in a household where the equivalent income (after housing costs) is less than 60 per cent of that of the national median (middle) income level. In the UK today the median (or middle) household income is around £25,000 (OECD 2011a). Households whose income is below £15,000 (60 per cent of £25,000) are considered to be in relative poverty. In 2008/09 the 60 per cent threshold was equivalent to a disposable income (after deducting tax and housing costs) of around £119 a week for a single adult or of around £288 per week for a couple with two dependent children under the age of 14 (Poverty Site 2010a).

According to Stewart and Hills (2005), levels of poverty in the UK started to decline during the 1970s but underwent sustained increases during the 1980s before levelling out during the 1990s and early 2000s. In the decades following the Second World War the benefits of economic growth tended to be shared across all income groups; but this was not the case during the 1980s where growth benefited the richest most and the poorest least (Stewart and Hills 2005). The consequences of unequal distribution of economic gain are shown in Figure 2.1. In the UK, the richest 10 per cent of the population have a third of the country's total income, while the poorest 10 per cent have about 1 per cent of the wealth. In fact, the income of the richest tenth is more than the income of all those on below-average incomes (i.e. the bottom 50 per cent) combined (Poverty Site, 2010a).

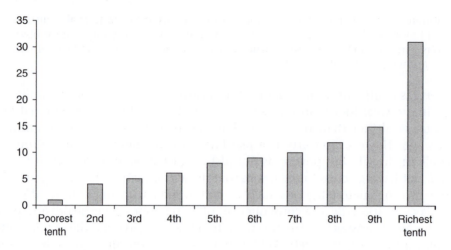

Figure 2.1   Share of total income according to poverty group, UK 2008/9

Source: Poverty Site (2010).

Over the last ten years, when house prices have (until recently) been rising and the economy experienced a period of rapid growth, the income of the poorest 10 per cent of the population has, in relative terms, been falling. At the same time, the richest 10 per cent of the population have seen a much bigger proportional rise in their income than any other group. Indeed, in 2008/9, 13.5 million people (about one fifth of the population) were living in households whose income was less than 60 per cent of the national median (Poverty Site 2010b).

Health Inequalities

> Reducing health inequalities is a matter of fairness and social justice … The fact that in England today people in different social circumstances experience avoidable differences in health, well-being and length of life is, quite simply, unfair. (Marmot Review 2010: 10)

The consequences of poor or failing health can be devastating for individuals, their families and society more widely. It is becoming increasingly common to read about the financial and social costs of an ageing population who, it is argued, will become increasingly dependent on the NHS. As well as the consequences for public health services of increased rates of obesity, heart disease and mental health problems among some social groups (for example, Smith et al. 2010; Department of Health 2010; Jotangia et al. 2006), perhaps what is most startling is the close relationship between health and socioeconomic status: what some experts term the 'social gradient' in health inequalities (Pickett and Dorling 2010; Smith et al. 2010). For the first time the poor are now, more likely than the rich, to be over weight (Wilkinson and Pickett 2010) and the challenges to public health for caring for an ageing, increasingly obese population are huge. Indeed, as we shall see in the second part of this chapter, childhood obesity and increased rates of mental illness among the young present a particular challenge.

Consider Figure 2.2. It shows that there are clear health inequalities – here exemplified by life expectancies – between men from different occupational classes. Those from 'professional' backgrounds (such as doctors and chartered accountants) are likely to live around eight years longer than those from 'unskilled' backgrounds (such as labourers and messengers). Similarly, people who live in poorer residential areas have lower life expectancy than those who live in more affluent areas. Even infant mortality rates are higher in families from lower socioeconomic groups (Department of Health 2010). According to some researchers these inequalities are increasing and although life expectancy is generally higher for everyone, the gap in mortality rates between those who live in the most and least wealthy districts continues to increase. There is even some evidence to suggest that these gaps are now the greatest since comparable data started to be collected in the 1920s (Thomas et al. 2010). In his recent book *Injustice*, Dorling gives the example of two women living in the same London borough. A woman aged 65 who lives in an affluent area could expect to live for about another 26 years, until she was around 90 years old. In contrast, a woman of the same age living in a poorer part of the same borough can expect to live for only another 12 years, until she was about 77 years old. This is just half as long as the woman who lives just a few miles away (Dorling 2010).

Health inequalities are not only linked to early death; similar patterns are reported in relation to chronic illnesses such as heart disease as well as in self-reports of well-being. Social surveys that ask people to rate how healthy

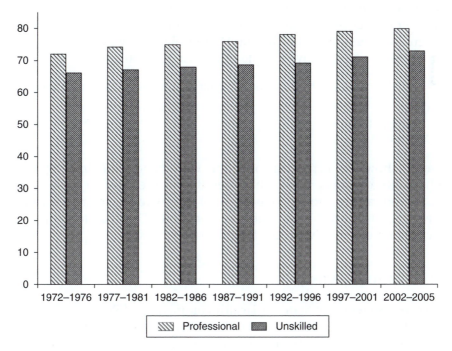

Figure 2.2   Life expectancy from birth for men from England and Wales, 1972–2005
Source: ONS (2007).

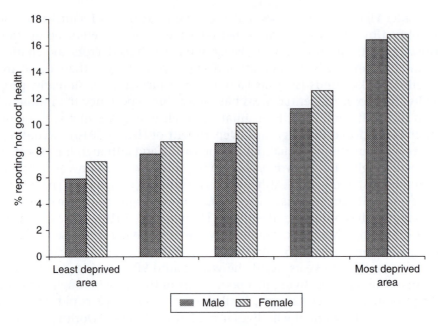

Figure 2.3   Self-reports of being in not good health among residents of private households in England by deprivation level and sex, 2001–5

Source: Smith et al. (2010).

they feel and whether or not they experience episodes of poor health reveal similar links between health and socioeconomic group. For example, between 2001 and 2005, the General Household Survey asked the following question to a representative sample of almost 100,000 adults:

Over the last 12 months would you say your health has on the whole been …

- Good
- Fairly good
- Not good

Figure 2.3 shows the percentage of people who report being in poor (i.e. not good) health according to whether they live in the most or least deprived areas. As you can see, around 16 per cent of men who live in areas with greatest deprivation reported their health as 'not good'. This is almost three times higher than men who live in the least deprived areas.

The Marmot Review

In 2008 the Secretary of State for Health commissioned Professor Sir Michael Marmot to undertake a review of the best evidence-based strategies to reduce health inequalities in England. The review, *Fair Society, Healthy Lives*, was published in February 2010, and further emphasised the link between *health* inequalities and *social* inequalities. To quote the report:

People with higher socioeconomic position in society have a greater array of life chances and more opportunities to lead a flourishing life. They also have better health. (Marmot Review 2010: 3)

Of the Review's six main recommendations (Marmot Review 2010: 9), two specifically relate to children and young people:

- Give every child the best start in life.
- Enable all children, young people and adults to maximise their capabilities and have control over their lives.

As priorities, the Review recommended increased investment in early years provision. This would include high-quality prenatal and maternity services, parenting programmes, childcare and early years education for all who need it. Among older children and young people they draw attention to the lasting impact of educational inequalities on physical and mental health and empha-sise that reducing educational inequalities is key to reducing other social ine-qualities including those relating to health. They suggest closer links between schools, families and the community and a focus on educating the 'whole child'.

The difficulty in deciding what is fair when it comes to improving public health can be neatly illustrated by looking at two different commentaries on Marmot's Review. The first perspective is offered by Canning and Boswer (2010). They argue that reducing health inequalities should not be the main goal, and instead that policies should be targeted at improving the health of everyone. They emphasise the need for more cost-effective, efficient and better-targeted health care for *all* 'so that health gains to the most advantaged are still considered beneficial in themselves, even though they increase health inequalities' (p. 1224). For them, reducing inequalities (in other words, the gap between the healthy rich and the sick poor) is not the priority; instead they wish to improve the health of everyone.

An alternative commentary is offered by Pickett and Dorling (2010). In contrast to Canning and Bowser, they are concerned that the Marmot Review did not go far enough in dealing with social inequalities in health. In their view 'it makes sense to target services to those who need them most, but even more sense to reduce the social inequalities that actually produce social dis-parities in health in the first place' (p. 1232). According to Pickett and Dorling (2010), one way of reducing these inequalities would be to curtail the excesses of the wealthy, for example through increased taxation of the super rich, the setting of a maximum income level or a constraint on the ratio of income between the highest and lowest earners.

So here are two perspectives on how best to reduce health inequalities:

- The first contends that policies should be aimed at improving the health of everyone and accepts that health inequalities are inevitable (an example of justice according to equality).
- The second perspective argues that any policies should promote the health of those who are in most need, and this tends to be the poorest sections of society. This would then reduce the equality gap between those in good health and those in less good health (an example of justice according to need).

Other Social Inequalities

Being poor is not simply about lacking material and economic resources. People who have less money are more likely to live in areas of high crime and be victims of crime themselves (Flatley et al. 2010; Lupton and Power 2005). They also tend to live in places that have the least favourable environmental conditions – such as poor housing, air quality and limited green space (DEFRA 2009). They are less likely to own a car or have access to the Internet (ONS 2009) and, as we saw in the previous section, are also more likely to have poor health. People who live in the most deprived areas spend around a quarter of their total gross income on housing costs (not including mortgage and council tax payments), compared to 6 per cent for those who live in affluent areas (ONS 2009).

Being poor also means that you are less likely to be able to afford the 'essential' items which one might expect for life in modern-day Britain. Figure 2.4 is taken from the government's Family Resources Survey and reported on the Poverty Site (2010c). As an example of the impact of being brought up in the poorest homes can have on the life experience of young children, it shows the percentage of children from low income families who do not experience an 'essential' activity, such as a family holiday or regular swimming lessons, because their parent(s) cannot afford it. As you can see, 60 per cent of children in the poorest homes went without an annual holiday because their parent(s) were unable to afford it, compared with 20 per cent of households whose

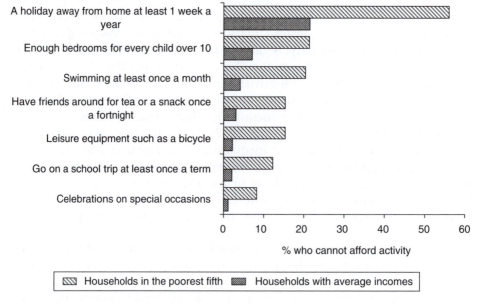

Figure 2.4 The proportion of children who do not have access to an 'essential' item because their parents cannot afford it

Source: Poverty Site (2010b).

income is at the average level. You may agree or disagree about whether these items are 'essential', but these items are those that more than half of the population say are essential for modern society. Other items which are considered to be 'essential' and which are most often lacking for people who live in poverty include having home contents insurance or two pairs of all-weather shoes.

International Comparisons Of Inequality

Of course, concern about unequal societies is not limited to the United Kingdom. Recent research by the OECD (Organisation for Economic Cooperation and Development, the group of the world's 34 richest nations) suggests that the income gap between the richest and the poorest people has grown over the last 20 years in most member countries (OECD 2010a). This brief section will highlight some of the inequalities that exist in countries that are similar, in economic terms, to the UK, for example France, Germany, Japan and the United States. If you are interested in reading more about global inequalities, particularly among developing nations, then a good place to start is with the Education for All programme. This is a global organisation led by UNESCO (United Nations Educational, Scientific and Cultural Organisation). It is dedicated to improving the educational opportunities of all children, youth and adults but has a particular focus on those who live in the poorer nations (UNESCO 2011).

Table 2.1 provides a comparison of rates of relative deprivation in a number of OECD member nations. It shows the percentage of households that experience a particular form of material deprivation, for example restricted access to health care or a healthy diet. You can see that even within these wealthy nations inequalities persist; for example, in the USA a third of households do not have access to a computer compared with just 2 per cent of Swedish households. Indeed it is not unusual to see the USA appearing towards the lower end of other similar measures of relative inequality (OECD 2008; see also Wilkinson and Pickett 2009 and Condron 2011). In the UK, while it is apparent that there are households that are experiencing high levels of deprivation, the national rates do not seem to be appreciably higher than those in economically similar countries.

Table 2.1 Comparison of rates of deprivation among selected OECD countries

Country	Households that are deprived in terms of			
	Restricted access to health care	Inability to have a healthy diet	Inability to make ends meet	Access to a computer
France	4	4	12	11
Germany	3	3	9	18
Ireland	10	10	10	15
Japan	2	n/a	25	12
Sweden	3	2	5	4
United Kingdom	3	3	7	10
United States	8	8	15	33

Source: OECD (2008: chapter 7).

Why does Inequality Matter?

In their 2009 book *The Spirit Level: Why Equality Is Better for Everyone*, Richard Wilkinson and Kate Pickett argue that 'at almost all levels of income, it is better to live in a more equal place' (p. 84). Countries with high levels of income inequality (where there are large gaps between the earnings of the richest and poorest citizens) are also likely to have more health and social problems, such as higher levels of mental illness, teenage births, homicide and imprisonment rates. This is illustrated in Figure 2.5. The USA has a high level of income inequality, and this is reflected in higher rates of social and health problems than exist in more equal countries such as Japan, Sweden and Norway.

Wilkinson and Pickett argue that it is not whether a country is wealthy or not that matters (average incomes are similar in the USA and Norway), rather it is how (un)equally this income is distributed among the population. In order to remedy the sorts of social and health problems that are listed here (and I could add many others, including educational inequalities) Wilkinson and Pickett argue that it is necessary to reduce the level of inequality in society – in other words to make society more equal. And the key to doing this is to reduce inequalities in the amount that people earn. There are two ways that they suggest governments might do this. They could make sure that the gaps in how much people earn are smaller than they are at the moment. This is what happens in Japan where wage

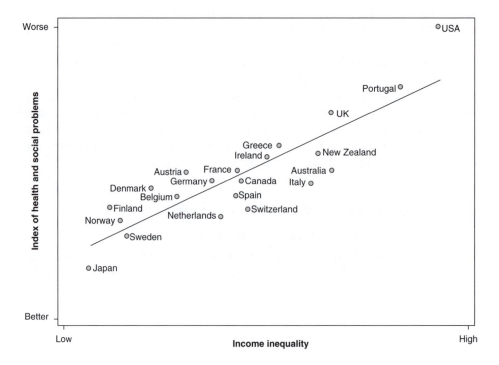

Figure 2.5 Health and social problems are closely related to inequality among rich countries
Source: ONS (2007).

differences are relatively small. Or they could distribute income among the population through increased taxation and benefits. This would mean that high wage earners pay a larger proportion of their income in taxes that are then used to fund social and other programmes in order to make society more equal. This is similar to what happens in Sweden and other Scandinavian countries.

There are of course several alternative arguments to Wilkinson and Pickett's proposals.[1] For example, proponents of Thatcherism would argue that people have the right to be unequal (remember Thatcher's 'tall poppies' speech from Chapter 1), that they have the right to work hard, earn a good wage and do better than their neighbours, and consequently that not all inequalities are unfair (think of the *justice as desert* argument). Indeed, there are many who might argue that the inequalities that we describe in this chapter are inevitable (and even desirable) in a modern market-led society, which creates incentives for people to work hard, earn more and so contribute to the country's overall economic growth (Platt 2011). There is also a widely held disregard for those who some would describe as the 'feckless' or 'undeserving' poor, those who George Osborne, the current Chancellor, criticised recently for taking the 'lifestyle choice to just sit on out-of-work benefits' (BBC 2010b). This is a view that is widely held (see BBC 2010c; Hutton 2010) and can be illustrated by the following comment that was posted on the discussion board of a national newspaper in response to the Marmot Review:

> The poor I know spend more on their cat and dog's food than their children's food, many of them smoke, drink and go to the betting shop. It's not about how much money you have, it's about how you spend it. (*Daily Mail*, VJB, London, 11/2/2010, 3:29)

Childhood and Inequality

Social inequalities and social exclusion do not just affect adults. In this section we will look at what recent evidence tells us about relative levels of child poverty and well-being in the world's wealthiest nations. Since 2000 tackling child poverty has become an important issue on the European Union's Social Policy Agenda and is the focus of numerous research studies and reports (for example, European Social Protection Committee, 2008; Bradshaw 2009). It is also embedded in the UN Convention on the Rights of the Child, Article 27 of which states that governments must

> ... recognise the right of every child to a standard of living adequate for the child's physical, mental, spiritual, moral and social development.

It also makes it clear that parents or others responsible for the child

> have the primary responsibility to secure ... the conditions of living necessary for the child's development...

... but that governments should assist parents

to implement this right and shall in case of need provide material assistance and support programmes, particularly with regard to nutrition, clothing and housing. (UNICEF 2011)

Despite these undertakings, millions of children, in even the world's wealthiest countries, continue to be born into and brought up in relative poverty. For example, in the European Union in 2005 around 19 million children, or 19 per cent of the total population aged 0–17, were living in poverty. In most EU countries, children are at a greater risk of living in poverty than the rest of the population (Bradshaw 2009; European Social Protection Committee 2008) and children who are brought up in lone-parent households or in large families (with three or more children) are also more likely to be poor. As we saw in the previous section, the consequences of living in poverty extend far beyond the ability to purchase the latest new product. Growing up in poverty is more likely to have a negative impact on a child's cognitive and behavioural development (Kiernan and Mensah 2009) and there is also a strong relationship between severe child poverty and parents' educational attainment (Magadi and Middleton 2007; Goodman et al. 2009). Evidence from the 1970 Birth Cohort Study (see Box 2.1) suggests that children from different social classes are already stratified in tests of intellectual and personal development at 22 months, a gap which becomes wider by age 10 (Feinstein 2003). The same study also finds no evidence 'that entry into schooling in any way overcame the polarisation of children's educational achievement linked to the deepening effects of parental background' (Feinstein 2003: 3; see also Kiernan and Mensah 2011; Goodman et al. 2009; Feinstein et al. 2008).

Box 2.1 How might we understand patterns of inequality?

One way to study whether poverty and other inequalities reproduce themselves from generation to generation is to study a cohort of people throughout their life course. There are a number of studies in the UK which do just this. One of the earliest British cohort studies with a focus on education was the National Child Development Study. This study collects information on the social, economic, physical and educational development of around 17,000 people who were born during a single week in 1958 and provides a unique resource for studying changes in British life over the last 50 years. Another cohort study, the 1970 British Cohort Study, has followed the lives of a similar number of children born in the same week in April 1970. The Millennium Cohort Study has followed 18,000 children who were born in the UK at the start of this millennium. The next round of data collection for the Millennium Cohort Study is planned for 2012 when the children will be 12 years old. Cohort studies like those described here enable researchers to study topics such as child behaviour, cognitive development, parenting styles, residential mobility, education and employment. In this way they can monitor children's development in different types of families and, as the children get older, their educational and employment trajectories. This can help them understand the influence that families and other social and cultural factors have on an individual's life chances and experiences and also the extent to which any differences are reproduced across generations. A good resource for finding out more about UK and international cohort studies is the 'Our Changing Lives' website (http://www.ourchanginglives.net/). The second volume of findings to emerge from the Millennium Cohort Study has recently been published as *Children of the 21st Century: The First Five Years* (Hansen et al. 2010).

Figure 2.6 shows the percentage of children who live in poverty in several OECD nations. It tells us that in the USA over 20 per cent of children live below the poverty line, compared with less than 5 per cent in Nordic countries such as Denmark and Finland. The poverty measure used here is *relative* poverty, defined according to how much a household's income is below the national median (middle) wage. However, using a measure of relative poverty leaves researchers open to the criticism that they are not measuring 'real'

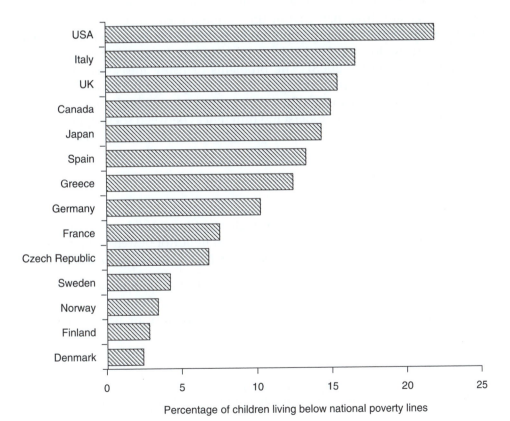

Percentage of children living below national poverty lines

Figure 2.6   Child poverty, selected OECD countries

Source: UNICEF (2005: table 1).

poverty at all. So, for example, a household can enjoy a relatively high standard of living, certainly in historical terms and in comparison with many in developing nations, while still bringing home less income than much of the rest of the population and so be defined as 'poor'. Indeed around 60 per cent of those living in 'poverty' in the UK are homeowners (BBC 2005). In the same way, international comparisons of poverty do not account for differences in national wealth. Take a look again at Figure 2.6. While the child poverty rate for children in the USA may be higher than that of the Czech Republic this does not mean that Czech children are more affluent than those in the USA. Instead it tells us that the Czech Republic has a more equal distribution of income than the USA. So in the Czech Republic people may well be poorer than they are in the USA but the difference between the rich and poor (i.e. relative poverty) is less in the Czech Republic than it is in America. So these figures tell us something about inequality within a nation but little about absolute levels of poverty and deprivation (UNICEF 2007).

Another problem with using indicators based solely on income is that they neglect other aspects of well-being that may have nothing to do with money. So a child who might be suffering from acute material deprivation because of their parents' alcohol or drug abuse is not counted as poor if their family income is greater than half that of the national median (UNICEF 2007). In this example, material deprivation might be a lack of access to good quality food, no television or an inadequately heated home (European Social Protection Committee 2008). The problems of using measures of poverty alone to understand disadvantage and inequality have been widely argued (see Magadi and Middleton 2007) and many indicators now include a number of other measures to help understand differences between social groups. One of these measures takes into account an individual's well-being (OECD 2009).

Child Well-being

According to the OECD (2009: 24), child well-being measures 'the quality of children's lives'. However, capturing a single measure of child well-being in just one indicator is very difficult. In developing an indicator of well-being researchers have to take into account a number of different factors, for example:

- *health* – such as immunisation rates, children's health behaviour;
- *subjective well-being* – such as experiences of health, enjoyment of school;
- *personal relationships* – such as self-reported quality of peer and family relationships;
- *material resources* – such as households in poverty or lack of access to 'essential' items;
- *education* – such as achievement and participation rates;
- *behaviour and risks* – such as involvement in violence, use of alcohol and drugs;
- *housing and the environment* – such as household overcrowding, living in high crime areas.

Table 2.2 Average rank on index of child well-being, selected OECD countries

Dimensions of child well-being	Average ranking (for all 6 dimensions)	Dimension 1 Material well-being	Dimension 2 Health and safety	Dimension 3 Educational well-being	Dimension 4 Family and peer relationships	Dimension 5 Behaviours and risks	Dimension 6 Subjective well-being
Netherlands	4.2	10	2	6	3	3	1
Sweden	5.0	1	1	5	15	1	7
Denmark	7.2	4	4	8	9	6	12
Finland	7.5	3	3	4	17	7	11
Spain	8.0	12	6	15	8	5	2
Switzerland	8.3	5	9	14	4	12	6
Norway	8.7	2	8	11	10	13	8
Italy	10.0	14	5	20	1	10	10
Ireland	10.2	19	19	7	7	4	5
Belgium	10.7	7	16	1	5	19	16
Germany	11.2	13	11	10	13	11	9
Canada	11.8	6	13	2	18	17	15
Greece	11.8	15	18	16	11	8	3
Poland	12.3	21	15	3	14	2	19
Czech Republic	12.5	11	10	9	19	9	17
France	13.0	9	7	18	12	14	18
Portugal	13.7	16	14	21	2	15	14
Austria	13.8	8	20	19	16	16	4
Hungary	14.5	20	17	13	6	18	13
United States	18.0	17	21	12	20	20	-
United Kingdom	18.2	18	12	17	21	21	20

Data only available for selected OECD counties (for example insufficient data are available for Japan, Australia).

Source: UNICEF (2007:2).

These seven factors (and you may be able to think of others that ought to be included) have also been combined by the OECD to provide one overall measure, or indicator, of well-being. They are concerned with what is happening to young people now (rather than with what might happen in the future) and in accordance with the UN Convention on the Rights of the Child they also represent what children 'say and think about their lives' (Bradshaw and Richardson 2009: 321; see also Rees et al. 2010; Thomas 2009; OECD 2009). Table 2.2 shows how many of the world's wealthiest nations (in term of their Gross Domestic Product) perform on an overall measure of well-being and also on six of the seven different factors that are listed above (*housing and the environment* are not included here).

In Table 2.2, countries that are highlighted with a dark background are placed in the bottom third (i.e. have the lowest scores on the indicators of well-being), a light background shows a place in the top third and mid-colour a place in the middle third. So a country like the Netherlands tops this table of child well-being and scores in the top ten for each of the six indicators. However, there is variation in the rankings for each of the indicators. For example, Sweden is ranked in the top third for five indicators, but for the sixth, family and peer relationships, it scores in the bottom third. These sorts of variation are partly a problem with ranking scores (look at how close the average scores are between Poland (12.3) and the Czech Republic (12.5)), but also show the difficulty of developing one single indicator of child well-being. Perhaps of greatest interest to many readers is the position of the UK – in this table it is ranked last and has the lowest scores on three out of the six indicators. Despite spending more money on children than most OECD countries, it appears that the UK still lags behind on some indicators of childhood inequality (OECD 2009). Indicators of well-being can only tell us so much, however. As with poverty, well-being is difficult to define and to measure consistently (Thomas 2009) and currently there is limited information on the depth and duration of child poverty or on more extreme forms of poverty (Magadi and Middleton 2007). There is a need for more research to further our understanding of the links between material deprivation, income poverty and the cycles of poverty, worklessness and exclusion that can affect generations (UNICEF 2007).

 Reflection: What is well-being?

Consider the following questions about indicators of well-being:

- What do you understand by the term well-being?
- What do you consider to be the challenges of measuring well-being in the way suggested in Table 2.2?

Child Poverty in the UK

In the UK in 2008/9, 3.9 million children were living in poverty. As discussed earlier, poverty is defined as those families whose earnings (after housing costs) are less than 60 per cent the median (middle) national income. In 2008/9 this was equivalent to £288 per week for a couple with two dependent children under 14 (Poverty Site 2010a). A stricter measure of severe poverty sets the threshold at 50 per cent of the median national income; this is equivalent to a weekly income of around £132 for a couple with one child. Indeed, the organisation Save the Children suggests that 1.7 million children across the UK live in severe poverty; this is around 13 per cent of all UK children (Magadi and Middleton 2007).

Children who live in poverty in the UK today are more likely to come from families headed by a lone parent, where there are three or more siblings (often aged under five), and where parent(s) do not work full-time. Child poverty rates are also higher in certain parts of the country (in the North East, Inner London and Wales, for example), in families from certain ethnic minority groups (especially Bangladeshi and Pakistani families) and where either the child or parent has a disability (Bradshaw 2009; Magadi and Middleton 2007). This is not to say that, for example, only workless families headed by a lone parent are at risk of poverty; it is actually the case that most children in poverty (62 per cent) are in two-parent families (but this is simply because most families have two parents). Even working full-time on the minimum wage and receiving all the in-work benefits and tax credits that are available is no guarantee that a child will not be brought up in a family whose income is below the poverty threshold (Bradshaw 2009). For those children who live in poverty, and particularly in severe poverty, it is not only that they are less likely to go on family holidays or are able to have friends around for tea or take swimming lessons; they are also at greater risk of poor health, childhood obesity (see Figure 2.7) and low educational attainment (Kiernan and Mensah 2011; Wilkinson and Pickett 2009). They are even at greater risk of injury on the roads (BBC 2010d).

In 1999, the Blair government pledged to halve child poverty in the UK by 2010 and to eradicate it by 2020. Even though there was a fall in the number of children living in poverty between 1998/9 and 2004/5, it looks as if the 2010 target will fall short by 600,000 children (Hirsch 2009). As you can see from Figure 2.8, there has been no overall reduction in child poverty since 2004, and in 2008 30 per cent of UK children were living in homes whose income was below the poverty line (with 20 per cent of children living in severe poverty). Only time will tell what impact the current financial crisis will have on levels of child poverty in the UK.

According to the last Labour government, 'the best way to tackle child poverty is to widen opportunities for parents to work, and raise the incomes of working families' (DfES 2003a: 25). In order to achieve this they introduced numerous initiatives to help parents into work, such as the New Deal, widening access to childcare, the introduction of the minimum wage and working family tax credits. They also provided additional financial support for families on low income, for those with very young children and for parents of disabled children, through initiatives such as the child tax credit (DfES 2003a). To some extent these policies appear to have worked and the number of poor children who live in households where no one works has decreased

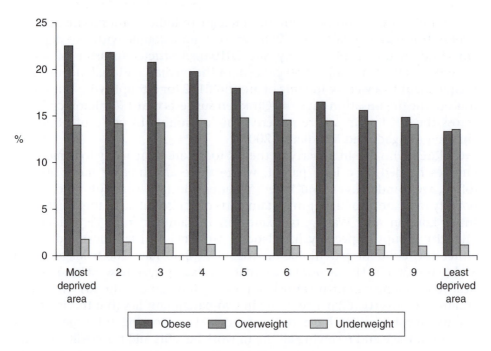

Figure 2.7 Prevalence of underweight, overweight and obese children aged 10–11 by school area deprivation, England, 2008/9

Source: Health and Social Care Information Centre (2009: figure 14).

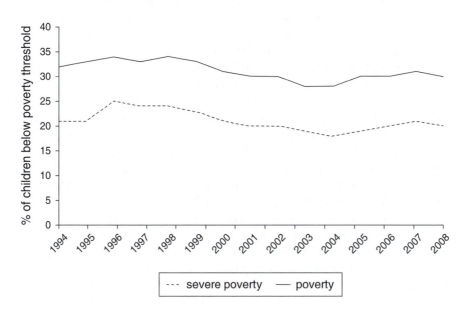

Figure 2.8 Percentage of children living below poverty thresholds, UK 1995–2008

Source: Department for Work and Pensions (2010).

since 1997, although the number of poor children living in working house-holds has hardly changed (Cooke and Lawton 2008). Indeed, according to the Innocenti Report on child poverty (UNICEF 2007), the number of children living in the most severe forms of poverty has been reduced in the UK, suggesting that policies to reduce child poverty appear to have benefited the poorest most.

Early Intervention Programmes to Reduce Childhood Inequalities

For as long as we have recognised social inequalities, there have been initiatives that seek to ensure that they do not persist from generation to generation, and in particular to try to ensure that young children begin their education with as few differences as possible. In June 2010 the then Prime Minister, Gordon Brown, commissioned Frank Field (the former Labour Minister for Welfare Reform and more recently the 'poverty czar') to undertake a review on the effect of poverty on life chances. The review, which reported in December 2010, concluded that if we are to prevent 'poor children becoming poor adults' then greater attention needs to be paid to the early stages of a child's life: 'Children's life chances are most heavily predicated on their development in the first five years of life' (Field 2010, 5). It recommended that the government invest greater funding into early years provision, particularly for the disadvantaged, and place a greater emphasis on providing high-quality and consistent support for parents throughout pregnancy and into early childhood. The most effective way to reduce inequalities in adult life outcomes, the report argues, is to introduce long-term strategies for 'narrowing the gaps in outcomes between poorer and richer children in the Foundation Years' (p. 50). Strategies to achieve this would involve high-quality integrated services involving parents and community partners. One initiative highlighted in the report is the Sure Stare Children Centres, which Field argues are crucial to the reform of early years provision. Sure Start is a flagship Labour initiative aimed to reduce exactly the sort of inequalities that Field raises in his report.

Sure Start

Sure Start Local Programmes (SSLP) were established between 1999 and 2003 as part of the Labour government's commitment to reducing child poverty and social exclusion (Home Office 1998). Their central aim was to enhance the life chances of young children and their families by improving services in areas of high deprivation. Specifically, they provided integrated community-based support in order to meet the following objectives:

- improving social and emotional development;
- improving health;
- improving children's ability to learn;
- strengthening families and communities.

Developed along similar lines to the Head Start programme in the USA (http://www.nhsa.org), Sure Start was intended to provide support that was specific to local needs including: outreach and home visiting; support for families and parents; support for good quality play, learning and childcare; primary and community healthcare; and support for children and parents with special needs (DCSF 2008). By 2005 there were 524 Sure Start Local Programmes (SSLPs) in England. From 2006 they started to function as Sure Start Children's Centres funded by local authorities. A series of evaluations into the effectiveness of Sure Start have been undertaken over the last ten years. It is too soon to have clear evidence about Sure Start's long-term impact but initial findings have been mixed. One of the most recent evaluations, which looked at 9,000 three year olds and their families in 150 areas, reached the following conclusion:

> after taking into consideration pre-existing family and area characteristics, comparisons of children and families living in SSLP areas with those living in similar areas not receiving SSLPs revealed a variety of beneficial effects for children and families living in SSLP areas, when children were 3 years old. (NESS 2008: v)

The evaluation also found better social development and behaviour among children living in Sure Start areas compared to those that did not, along with more examples of positive parenting and higher levels of engagement with family support services. More recent evaluations point towards improved physical health as well as less chaotic and more cognitively stimulating home environments for young children living in SSLP areas (NESS 2010). However, these somewhat positive outcomes were in contrast to the findings from earlier evaluations that appeared to suggest that the most disadvantaged three year olds and their families were doing less well in SSLPs (NESS 2005). There are several possible reasons that might explain such contradictory findings; they may be related to the research methods used or accounted for by the more recent evaluation taking place in more mature and long running programmes (NESS 2008). A large recent study undertaken by Christine Merrell and Peter Tymms at Durham University points to the long-term stability of young children's performance in baseline assessments of reading, vocabulary and mathematics. This is despite the large number of initiatives, such as Sure Start, that aim to improve basic skills in the early years. However, it is important to note that in this study the researchers were not evaluating Sure Start programmes directly (Merrell and Tymms 2010).

In his report into childhood inequality, Frank Field argued that Sure Start was fundamental to any reform of early childhood (Field 2010). Although recommending a fundamental change in the way in which the programme operates, he nevertheless viewed Sure Start as crucial in narrowing class-based educational differences that children from disadvantaged areas may arrive with in school. However, in October 2010, the Coalition government announced a series of cuts to public spending. While Ministers have maintained that these cuts will not affect Sure Start, its future does remain uncertain. For example, in previous years funds that are given to local authorities to pay for Sure Start have been ring-fenced (i.e. they can only be used to fund Sure Start and not for other programmes). This has now been changed and Sure Start will be funded through a new Early Intervention Grant (EIG), that will also be used to fund other early intervention and preventative services such as Connexions, the Youth Opportunity Fund and the Early Years sustainability programme (DfE 2010a; 2011a; BBC 2010e). Although funding for Sure Start will remain the same, funding for the EIG has been reduced by 11 per cent and recent estimates reported by the BBC suggest that at least one Sure Start Centre in each English local authority is likely to close because of funding cuts (BBC 2011a; Butler 2011; Ward 2011).

Box 2.3 Sure Start Children's Centres in action

McNay Street Children's Centre is located in the town of Darlington in the North East of England. The area in which the centre is located is characterised by high levels of deprivation and in comparison with the town itself has a high proportion of residents who claim benefits and who report incidents of poor health (ONS 2011). The centre provides childcare and educational courses as well as family support and child and family health services. It also provides links to Job Centres and training providers and offers advice on entering the workforce as well as basic skills training and information on managing finances. McNay Street Children's Centre has over twenty specialist staff including health visitors, community health nurses, a breast-feeding coordinator, a fathers' worker/parental engagement officer and several Early Years Practitioners. There is more information about the Children's Centre's work at http://www.mcnay-street.childrencentre.org.

Summary

This has been a very brief introduction to a hugely important area of social research. It is impossible to cover all aspects of this topic in such a short chapter and I hope that you will follow the links to the additional resources and reading in order to explore this area in more detail yourself. This chapter has hopefully introduced you to the idea that the inequalities that we concern ourselves with in the field of education are also present in wider society:

in the different types of neighbourhoods where people live, in how much money they earn, in their health and also in their well-being. Inequalities that are present among the adult population are often replicated among the young. The important question for those interested in education is to what extent can education – and schooling in particular – mitigate these background factors? Indeed, 'how to educate the poor?' is possibly the greatest challenge facing educationalists today.

 Reflection

According to the philosopher Basil Bernstein, 'education cannot compensate for society'. Consider the other social inequalities that we have covered in this chapter and the vast funds that are put into initiatives such as Sure Start. To what extent do you think that Bernstein's statement is true today?

Note

1. If you are interested in exploring this further I would encourage you also to read Peter Saunders' *Beware False Prophets* (Saunders 2010) in which he presents a counter-argument to that given in *The Spirit Level*. Read them both and make up your own mind.

Additional resources

The EHRC report on fairness

The Equality and Human Rights Commission's (EHRC) triennial report on fairness in Britain was published in 2010. The report summarises the progress that the country has made towards becoming a fairer society in terms of education, health, housing, standards of living, security and people's voice. The EHRC's website (http://www.equalityhumanrights.com) provides full access to the report, including case studies and a video introduction.

The Equality Trust

The Equality Trust is a non-partisan organisation established in 2009 by the authors of *The Spirit Level* and their colleagues. Its stated aims are to reduce income inequality through a programme of public and political education designed to achieve:

- a widespread understanding of the harm caused by income inequality;
- public support for policy measures to reduce income inequality;
- the political commitment to implementing such policy measure.

Its website (http://www.equalitytrust.org.uk) acts as a companion to the book as well as providing access to other publications, video and audio clips, blogs and campaigning resources.

Gapminder

Gapminder is a wonderful website which uses Trendalyzer software to display statistical time series as colourful interactive graphs. The website brings together data from international organisations such as the World Health Organisation, the OECD and the United Nations. The interactive software allows you to easily plot graphs which can show long-term trends and relationships between a whole range of different variables covering topics such as health, economy, education, environment and work.

The Poverty Site

The Poverty Site is a very useful resource for those interested in poverty and social exclusion in the UK. It provides access to the latest data on poverty as well as on the other indicators that were introduced in this chapter plus many more: health, crime, housing, education, disability and ethnic minorities. It can be accessed at http://www.poverty.org.uk.

Further reading

Dorling, D. (2010) *Inequality*. Bristol: Policy Press.

Hansen, K., Joshi, H. and Dex, S. (eds) (2010) *Children of the 21st Century: The First Five Years*. Bristol: Policy Press.

Hutton, W. (2010) *Them and Us: Changing Britain – Why We Need a Fair Society*. London: Little Brown.

Rees, G., Goswami, H. and Bradshaw, J. (2010) *Developing an Index of Children's Subjective Well-being in England*, Report for the Children's Society. Available from http://www.childrenssociety.org.uk.

Wilkinson, R. and Pickett, K. (2009) *The Spirit Level: Why Equality Is Better for Everyone*. London: Penguin Books.

3

Good schools for all: schooling and social justice

> Let the reader reflect on the present life of hundreds of thousands of boys and girls, on the prevalence of physical ailments among them, on their premature overwork, on their hurried and truncated schooling, on the waste of capacity caused by the failure to make smooth the way to higher education ... and he will not think it extravagant to suggest that they should be educated up to sixteen under the most favourable conditions that the progress of educational science can offer.
>
> (R. H. Tawney 1922: 147)

As the above quotation shows, the ideal of good schools for all students is not new. For example, it was central to R. H. Tawney's call, in the years following the First World War, for the development of public secondary education for all 'irrespective of the income, class or occupation of their parents' (1922: 7). It was present in both the 1944 Education Reform Act and in the 1965 Education Act that approved the reorganisation of secondary education along comprehensive lines in order to 'preserve all that is valuable in grammar school education for those children who now receive it and make it available to more children' (DES 1965).

   In this chapter we consider the extent to which the ideal of good quality schools for all children is still in evidence today. This is a large and important topic for which a short chapter like this can only hope to provide an introduction. In this brief excursion through some of the topic's key issues we consider the importance of international comparisons of educational attainment along with national policies that have played an important part in shaping school reform in recent years. We look in particular at the two lynchpins of current school policy in England: Academies and free schools. We begin with a consideration of the role of schooling in promoting social justice.

Schooling and Social Justice

One feature of the education system in this country is the ever increasing diversity of its schools. For example there are schools that select young people on the basis of their family income, ability or faith; there are also schools that specialise in certain areas of the school curriculum (such as sport, science or languages) and state-funded schools that are able to operate outside the control of local authorities. Another feature of our current system is the rich vocabulary that has emerged to describe the shortcomings of our schools, their teachers and their pupils. Over the last twenty years or so we have read much about the 'sink schools' and 'bog standard comprehensives' that have been left behind while the affluent and able have been 'creamed off' to the selective sector. A great deal has been written about schools being 'named and shamed' and placed in 'special measures', of schools that are full of 'useless' teachers failing to teach the 'unteachable'. During the mid-1990s, schools such as the Ridings School in Yorkshire and Hackney Downs, the once venerable London Boys' Grammar School, became synonymous with the failure of many schools that were often located in the inner cities or other areas of socioeconomic disadvantage (for example, Barber 1995). That all schools are not the same and that all students' school experiences are not equal is well illustrated by the two extracts below. The first is taken from a letter to a national newspaper from the head teacher of a special school that had been notified of the Coalition government's plans to cease funding for the Building Schools for the Future programme. The second comes from the website of a large independent school and also describes the facilities available to its students.

> I work in a special school. For at least the past 15 years our school has been trying to move to new premises. Our buildings are hopelessly inadequate for our students, many of whom have severe learning difficulties and autism; more than 30% of the classrooms are temporary structures; corridors are not wide enough for wheelchairs; there is no medical room; staff have nowhere to prepare or meet; the hall, dining room and other essential areas are used for storage; there is a chronic lack of parking. No matter how good the teaching and learning is (and it is very good), we can never get the highest grades from Ofsted.

> The school is fortunate in its site, a beautiful 50 acre expanse ... The school's sporting facilities are also extensive. For indoor sport, the school has one large sports hall, two gymnasia, three squash courts, an indoor 25-metre swimming pool and a weight-training room. For outdoor sports ... two newly refurbished hockey astro pitches, a small astro pitch for hockey, football and tennis, and enough space in front of the school's main buildings for five rugby pitches in the winter and three cricket grounds in the summer. In addition, the school owns extensive land ... where it has the 1st XI cricket pitch, the 1st XV rugby pitch, an athletics track and tennis courts.

There are many reasons why we need an education system that is based on principles of social justice. The role of the school in ensuring equity for its pupils is important; education is not a final good. For example, schools have a responsibility to society for producing at least minimally qualified individuals. As the link between earnings and academic qualifications grows, so does an individual's stake in their education: how well someone does at school has become ever more strongly linked to the sort of job one will get and consequently how much money they will earn. Therefore education is increasingly seen as something the state owes to its citizens and arguably this means that it is the state's responsibility to ensure that the school system is fair (Meuret 2002).

In the UK, the state is still the main provider of a national education system that is largely funded by the taxpayer. As a result, ensuring a fair and equitable education system has political as well as social implications. One consequence of this is that schools are held publicly accountable for the performance of their students. In England, for example, this has resulted in systems of 'high-stakes testing' (these are tests which have important consequences for the test taker – an example would be A-levels which might decide which university they can go to) and punitive school accountability measures that make assessment results for individual schools publicly available, even for small primary schools that may have fewer than 30 students in a cohort. However, as the next section shows, in a globalised economic community where the stakes for educational underperformance are high, it is to the results of tests which compare student attainment in different nations that the critics of school standards increasingly turn (see, for example, Grek 2008).

International Comparisons of Educational Performance

One of the key drivers of school reform in many developed countries – and the UK is no exception here – is their performance in international comparative tests such as the Programme for International Student Assessment (PISA) and the Trends in International Maths and Science Study (TIMSS) (see Box 3.1 for a brief introduction to these tests). The results from the most recent round of PISA were released just weeks after the Coalition government published its first White Paper on education. They could hardly have been more timely:

> So much of the education debate in this country is backward looking: have standards fallen? Have exams got easier? These debates will continue, but *what really matters* is how we're doing compared with our international competitors. That is what will define our economic growth and our country's future. The truth is, at the moment we are standing still while others race past. (DfE 2010b: 1, emphasis added)

Through this opening paragraph of their new White Paper, the new Coalition government has reiterated the imperative that education is the cornerstone of an effective economy, or in other words that 'education is the best economic policy' (Brown 2007). And the relatively poor performance of British 15 year olds in PISA 2009 (OECD 2010b) has only served to reaffirm their dissatisfaction with the current domestic school system.

The increasing popularity of sophisticated comparative tests such as PISA and TIMSS has enabled nations to look critically at the performance of their schools in comparison with their international neighbours. This has led to many nations re-examining their education systems in light of perceived failings in these comparative assessments. In many countries – and again the UK is no exception here – this has been used to further justify dissatisfaction with the domestic school system and has led to accusations of falling academic standards and failing pupils. An excellent example of the consequences that 'low' test scores can have for a nation's education system is Germany. Their relatively poor performance in PISA 2000 resulted in radical reform of the education system leading to the introduction of new assessment frameworks, school inspection regimes and other measures of educational quality and accountability (Grek 2008; Ertl 2006). In contrast to the 'PISA-shock' felt by Germany, there is the 'PISA-surprise' experienced by Finland who topped the PISA league tables. Finland's relative success in these assessments has attracted much international praise and attention and has been attributed to a highly regarded teaching profession, a conservative pedagogy and comprehensive school system (Simola 2005).

So why do these tests get so much attention? One key reason is apparent in the above quotation: the presumed link between better schools and a better economy. Economic globalisation has meant that many semi-skilled jobs have moved out of Western nations and into countries such as China. This has resulted in countries such as the UK and USA needing to refocus their economic priorities and to develop a more highly qualified and technically competent workforce. And that, according to many politicians, is the job of the schools. Perhaps then it is not surprising that the intensity of scrutiny given to nations' relative performance in these tests has contributed to the 'crisis account' of failure that is apparent in many Western nations (Brown 1998; Grek 2008). However, it is also interesting to see how quickly these perspectives change. Britain's previous relative success in these tests had been attributed to a return to traditional teaching methods in primary schools (*Daily Mail*, 7 April 2003), the National Literacy Strategy (*Guardian*, 9 April 2003) and even to Harry Potter (*Daily Express*, 9 April 2003). On the other hand, the apparent failure of schools in England in the more recent rounds of PISA has been regarded by some sectors of the British press to mark a failure of Labour's education policies (*London Evening Standard*, 6 December 2007; *Financial Times*, 5 December 2007), the fault of trendy teaching methods and a dumbed-down exam system (*Daily Mail*, 8 December 2010), the consequences of which are to leave one in five students 'stranded on the rocks of life' when they leave school (*Times Educational Supplement*, 17 December 2010).

International tests are expensive, they are complex to design and administer, their focus is relatively narrow and much care needs to be taken with their interpretation. Education systems are changing and evolving, government policy shifts in its priorities, and the different contexts in which education systems operate can also change. These and many other factors have

Table 3.1   Programme for International Student Assessment 2009, selected countries

Country	Reading score	Performance gap[a]	Lowest performers[b] (%)	'Equity' gap[c]
Korea	539	200	6	69
Finland	536	223	8	61
Canada	524	231	10	67
Japan	520	253	14	75
US	500	253	18	107
Sweden	497	252	17	91
Germany	497	248	18	105
Ireland	496	238	17	85
France	496	272	20	110
UK	494	246	18	93
Italy	486	246	21	84
Spain	481	224	20	82
Czech Republic	478	241	23	84
OECD country average	493	241	19	89

[a]Performance gap is the difference in the scores between the highest and lowest 10 per cent.
[b]Lowest performers are those who scored below expected proficiency levels.
[c]Equity gap is the gap between the lowest and highest 25per cent of pupils on the PISA index of economic, social and cultural status.

Source: OECD (2010b, 2010c).

to be taken into account when we examine the relative performance of students nationally and especially internationally (see, for example, Brown 1998; Smith 2005a; Gorard and Smith 2010). To put this in some context, Table 3.1 shows how several nations scored in the 2009 PISA tests of reading literacy.

This table tell us several things about the UK performance in PISA 2009 relative to other nations:

- With an average reading score of 494, the UK scores at the average level for OECD countries but lower than leading scorers such as Finland and Korea. Note, however, how closely the scores are clustered together from the US at 500 down to the UK at 494.
- The gap between the scores of the highest and lowest performing students is relatively narrow in Korea (200 points) but widest in France (272 points). The gap for the UK is around the average for all countries but still reflects a wide difference in attainment between students.
- Further differences in the relative attainment of UK students in PISA are reflected in the final two columns of Table 3.1. First they show that around 18 per cent of UK students do not achieve basic levels of proficiency in reading. A second is that when social and cultural background factors are taken into account, there is a gap of 93 points in the performance of the 'least' and 'most' advantaged students.

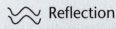 Reflection

Look closely at the UK's scores in comparison to those for other mid-ranking countries such as Germany, France and Sweden. To what extent do the patterns for UK students differ to those of these other nations?

Box 3.1 What are PISA, TIMSS and PIRLS?

The answer is that they are all international comparative tests of, among other things, academic attainment. Each is described briefly here along with references for further reading.

The Programme for International Student Assessment (PISA) is a series of assessments that are taken by 15-year-old students and designed to 'assess student performance and collect data on the student, family and institutional factors that can help explain differences in performance' (OECD 2001: 4). PISA is administered by the Organisation for Economic Cooperation and Development (OECD) and students are assessed in three areas: Language, Mathematics and Science. PISA runs in three-yearly cycles and while each subject area is assessed in each cycle, one subject is given prominence. The first wave in 2000 focused mainly on Language, the second wave on Mathematics and the third on Science. The latest wave of PISA took place in 2009 focusing once more on Language. In 2009, around 470,000 students from 65 countries or economies participated in PISA. Data was collected on student background as well as on the characteristics of the schools that they attend. There is a great deal of information on all waves of PISA on the website http://www.oecd.org/PISA.

The Trends in International Mathematics and Science Study (TIMSS) differs from PISA in that rather than measuring how students apply knowledge to real-life problems, it focuses on topics that students are likely to have covered in school. It is carried out with students in National Curriculum Years 6 and 9, takes place every four years and, as its title suggests, focuses on Mathematics and Science. The first wave of TIMSS was in 1995 and the latest in 2011, with around 60 countries participating. Just like PISA, TIMSS is more than just a test; it also collects data on curriculum, classroom resources and teacher preparation. There is more information on the different waves of TIMSS at http://timssandpirls. bc.edu/.

The Progress in International Reading Literacy Study (PIRLS) collects data on the reading literacy attainment of National Curriculum Year 5 students. It investigates reading comprehension and also gathers information about reading experiences in the school and the home. PIRLS is administered every five years with the first assessment taking place in 2001. Over 50 countries participated in PIRLS 2011. For further information and publications about PIRLS, see http://timssand-pirls.bc.edu/.

Improving Schools

According to Gary Orfield, the Director of the Civil Rights Project at the University of California in Los Angeles, policy-makers' preoccupations with perceived mediocre performance in international tests of educational performance such as PISA have contributed to a refocusing of educational priorities in many Western countries. This has resulted in a movement away from policies that have attempted to resolve the inequities faced by poorer children – for example by increasing access to high-quality education, desegregating schools and reducing achievement gaps – and towards ones concerned with more testing, more accountability and increasingly market-driven systems of school choice (Orfield 2000). In the US context this has resulted in systems of high-stakes testing and strict school accountability sanctions, epitomised by the No Child Left Behind legislation (see below). In England, an already highly regulated and highly accountable national school system has experienced further moves towards increased diversity of provision driven by choice and market-based policies, all of which are set to continue under the new Coalition government. In the current political climate, where attention to 'fairness' and 'social justice' appears to be paramount, these reforms are ostensibly aimed at improving the educational experiences of those sections of the school population which have traditionally been the least academically successful. In this section we will explore two policies towards school improvement: increased parental choice and diversity of schooling. While our focus here will mainly be on England it is important to remember that the three other home nations – Wales, Scotland and Northern Ireland – have their own national debates around education. Some of these reflect what is happening in England (such as their responses to results of international tests) while others point to the increasing divergence of education policies in the four countries (such as the funding provision for higher education and national testing regimes), (see, for example, Daugherty 2009 and Phillips 2003.)

Parental Choice of Schools

One characteristic of school policy in England over the last 20 years or so has been the increased choice that parents have over deciding to which school to send their children. In large urban areas in particular this has resulted in increased competition for places in schools perceived to be the most 'successful', with some local authorities and councils resorting to using a lottery system to allocate school places in an attempt to make the system 'fairer' (Frean and Sugden 2008). There are different views on the impact that increased parental choice has had on the social characteristics of schools. Some researchers contend that more choice has led to increased social segregation with middle-class parents being better able to target places in the most successful schools (Reay and Ball 1998). An alternative perspective is offered by

Gorard et al. (2003) and Gorard and Fitz (2006). Their study of all secondary schools in England and Wales showed that in the immediate aftermath of policies to increase parental choice, schools actually became less segregated. This does not mean, of course, that schools in England and Wales are not socially segregated at all. They are. Rather it suggests that policies to create school markets where parents have greater choice cannot alone determine how segregated schools become (see also Coldron et al. 2010). Instead, it is demographic factors (often in terms of where you live) and socioeconomic factors (often in terms of how much you earn) which have a large effect on determining levels of segregation between schools. In addition, schools also tend to be more segregated in areas where there is a lot of diversity in school provision, so where faith, independent and other selective schools 'compete' with each other for students.

Reflection

One way in which parents exercise their right to choose their child's school is for them to opt out of the state school system completely in favour of the independent sector. In this chapter we focus only on the schooling of young people in state-maintained schools. Although this is where the majority of children and young people are taught, around 7 per cent are educated in the independent or private sector. To question whether parents should be able to pay for their child's education is arguably to question our democratic right as citizens to choose what we think is best for our families. However, it is nevertheless an important question and one that gets to the heart of many issues around justice and education.

In Chapter 1 we introduced some of John Rawls' views on justice. This is a theme which is taken up in Episode 8 of Michael Sandel's lecture series called 'Justice', from which the following questions are adapted (http://www.justiceharvard.org/). Have a look at the episode and then consider the following questions:

- Often poor children who are very talented have unequal opportunities because their parents lack the money to send them to good schools, to pay for private lessons and so on. Compared to equally talented children of rich parents, poor kids have fewer opportunities to develop their talents. Why might this be unjust?
- Rawls argues that talented and hard-working poor children should have the same chances of success as rich children. Do you agree with him? Suppose that providing equal educational opportunity for all children would require substantial taxes on the rich. After all, it would cost a lot of money to provide schools of the same quality to everyone. Do you believe that such taxes are required as a matter of justice?

Diverse Schools

One feature of contemporary school reform in England, in particular, has been the creation of diverse and autonomous schools. These schools allow freedom to innovate and to engage with business and enterprise and enable schools to develop their own ethos and specialisms. In short, a new type of school has emerged, one that is much less like the 'bog standard' comprehensives of old and much more likely to define its own identities of excellence and diversity. This is exemplified best in two recent initiatives: the academy schools programme and free schools.

The Academy Schools Programme

> I see academies as engines of social mobility and social justice: new schools of aspiration for all, striving for excellence in all that they do. (Lord Adonis, speech to the National Academies Conference, 7 February 2008)

Academies are state-funded schools that operate outside local authority control. In their original conception they were managed and governed by charitable companies comprised of sponsors from the business, education or voluntary sectors as well as from faith communities (NAO 2010). Labour opened the first three academies in 2002. These new schools were housed in iconic new buildings with state-of-the-art facilities. They had the independence to manage their own staff and to select a small proportion of their pupils on ability alone. By the time Labour left office in May 2010 there were 203 academies with a similar number in the planning stage. The academy schools programme is notable in that it received support from both main political parties, albeit for different reasons (Leo et al. 2010). One of the earliest actions of the new Education Secretary, Michael Gove, was to allow only those schools that Ofsted had designated as 'outstanding' to become academies. By November 2010 he had extended this to include all schools, provided they work in partnership with a high-performing school that will help drive improvement (DfE 2010c, 2010d). Indeed, it is evidence of the fervour with which the new Coalition government has embraced the academy movement that by May 2011 there were 658 academy schools open in England (DfE 2011b; BBC 2011b).

As Lord Adonis, one of the originators of the programme, suggests in the quotation above, academies were originally intended to provide 'all-ability schools with the capacity to transform the education of children in areas of disadvantage and need' (DfES 2001: 49). The early academies were indeed located in areas of high socioeconomic deprivation and low educational engagement. However the decision by Michael Gove to open up the academies programme to all schools arguably removes this undertaking to focus resources and excellence towards the most vulnerable.

There have been numerous criticisms of the academies programme. Many are ideological and reflect concerns that the taxpayer will be funding schools that are run and managed by largely unaccountable private sponsors (see, for example, Ball 2007; also West and Currie 2008, and the controversy that surrounded the Vardy Foundation's sponsorship of academies in the North East of England (Branigan 2002)). Indeed, the concept of the academy as a self-governing institution has also proven to be controversial. The original academies were not required to sign up to the national pay framework for teaching staff, meaning that they were free to set salary terms and conditions for their teachers (Tice 2008), as well as having the flexibility to select and exclude pupils that was not available to other schools (Curtis et al. 2008).

Now that the academies programme has been running for almost a decade and as the programme is being expanded to include all schools, it is worth examining the extent to which the original aims of the scheme have been met and whether academies are indeed at the 'the vanguard of meritocracy' (Adonis 2008) as their creators intended. However, evaluating the effectiveness of the academies programme is not straightforward: there are many different types of academy with many different types of sponsor, and some academies have only been operating for a relatively short period of time and so it is simply too early to measure progress reliably (see, for example, Curtis et al. 2008; Freedman 2010).

Nevertheless, according to a recent report from the National Audit Office (NAO 2010), most academies are achieving academic performance levels above those of the predecessor school, and are improving at a faster rate than equivalent schools. However, while the performance of pupils who receive free school meals (FSM) (in all schools, not just in academies) has improved over time, 'on average, the gap in attainment between more disadvantaged pupils and others has grown wider in Academies than in comparable maintained schools' (NAO 2010: 6). So this rise in overall achievement in academy schools appears to coincide with a decline in the number of disadvantaged students, as measured by receipt of FSM, who attend the schools. As one of the key aims of the academy programme was to improve the educational attainment of the most disadvantaged students, this is an important development. So far it appears that while there is 'no clear evidence to suggest that academies work to produce better results than the kinds of schools they replaced' (Gorard 2009: 112), there is some evidence to suggest that the early academies now educate lower proportions of young people who are eligible for FSM. There are two ways of viewing this trend:

- In order to meet league table targets academies are somehow adjusting their intake to recruit from more affluent (and potentially higher-attaining) families.
- Alternatively, that relatively affluent families who might previously have been put off sending their child to the local, possibly lower-attaining, 'bog standard' school have become attracted to the state-of-the-art facilities that the academy has to offer.

This second explanation could therefore be seen as a positive decision by parents to engage with the new schools. So more affluent families sending their children to the academy school would lead to an overall drop in the proportion of children eligible for FSM and the school would become more comprehensive (or mixed) in its intake (Gorard 2005, 2009).

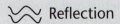 Reflection

The current policy that has seen all state schools invited to opt out of local authority control and become academies means that Labour's original intention of focusing the academy programme in areas of 'disadvantage and need' no longer holds. Do you think that this is fair?

There are two perspectives on this. One might argue that it is right that extra resources are devoted to schools that might be in greater need because they support vulnerable communities. On the other hand, what of the schools that because of their very success would not have qualified for an academy's additional funding and freedom to innovate? Is it fair that these 'successful' schools are denied opportunities that are available to less 'successful' schools? What do you think?

Free Schools

Despite the Coalition government's clear enthusiasm for the academies programme, their flagship school diversification policy is arguably the free school. Free schools are not a particularly new idea. You will find their equivalent in Sweden and in the USA (where they are called charter schools) where they have existed for many years with mixed levels of success (see, for example, Allen 2010 and Centre for Research on Education Outcomes 2009). Free schools are all-ability, state-funded independent schools, set up in response to parental demand (DfE 2011c). Like academies they will be free from local authority control. Their aim is to 'tackle educational inequality and to give greater power to parents and pupils to choose a good school' (DfE 2010c). By the beginning of February 2011, 41 applications for free schools had either been approved to open or were in the process of finalising their business case (DfE 2011c) and 24 free schools opened in September 2011.

In essence, free schools and academies are very similar. A key (and controversial) difference, however, is that while academies tend to be formed from existing schools, free schools can be completely new establishments set up in completely new premises. Supporters of free schools argue that the model provides parents with greater choice and that a more diverse and autonomous system will help raise standards (Millar and Young 2010). Opponents argue that they will result in further segregation of schools by attracting mainly middle-class parents who are dissatisfied with the state system. In addition, as free schools will require new facilities and new teachers, they will divert funding away from existing schools. This is particularly an issue in large urban areas, especially London, where pressure on school places and a culture of parental choice has long been an issue (Vincent et al. 2010). A report published by the Adam Smith Institute in April 2011 suggests that unlike the academy programme, which has attracted large numbers of new schools, the progress of free schools has, so far, been 'disappointing' (Croft, 2011: 5). The report continues to recommend that for free schools to succeed, they will need to operate on a for-profit basis.

Debate: What Schools for the Future?

One of the most prominent supporters of free schools outside the government is the author Toby Young. He is the founder of the West London Free School, the first free school to be approved by the government, which opened in September 2011. Melissa Benn is founder of the Local Schools Network and a champion of comprehensives. Their debate on whether the government's policy for free schools will raise standards or lead to a two-tier system was published in the *Guardian* on 5 February 2011. An abridged version appears below:

TY: In west London we want to start a school that is faithful to the original ideal of comprehensive schools ... grammar schools for all. At our school we want every child to study Latin up to age 14, and do at least six academic GCSEs ... The problem with the current system is that, by and large, in order to secure access to an academically rigorous education, you need to either be of the right faith, you need to live within the catchment area of a high-performing comprehensive, or you need to be able to afford to go private, and that's why social mobility has ground to a halt.

MB: I don't think that's true. Children in so-called ordinary comprehensives can get a good academic education. A really good comprehensive offers access to academic subjects, but it also offers access to other subjects, so that children of all types can learn together ... The effect of private schools, grammar schools and faith schools is that a lot of other schools are dealing with a high proportion of disadvantaged children ... I would like to see more money put into those schools, the best teachers in those schools – and I would like to see all selection phased out.

TY: I think we would both like to see fee-paying schools phased out. Wouldn't it be a fantastic result if enough parents and teachers set up outstanding secondary schools to which all children had access, so that fee-paying schools quietly went out of business?

MB: Look five years down the line and we might see a two-tier system within the state sector, where schools like yours become places the motivated middle classes flood to – in effect, grammar schools – and other schools, including some academies, will be de facto secondary moderns.

TY: ... I think we have a common aim, which is to reduce unfairness in the present system. Your solution is to reduce choice, mine is to increase it. Why should the state have a monopoly over the provision of taxpayer-funded education?

While we can argue about the principles of free schools we won't know what their effect will be for many years. A good way of understanding the impact of increased parental choice on schools systems is to take a look at the impact

of the charter school movement in the USA. Two useful websites are: http://
www.uscharterschools.org and http://www.nea.org/home/16332.htm.

Arguably more fundamental than questions about what policy-makers can
do to improve schools is the question of what makes a good school. Perhaps
surprisingly, this is a very difficult one to answer. Two perspectives on this are
introduced here.

What Makes a Good School?

That schools matter and can have a major impact upon children and young
people's development is characteristic of an area of work called school effectiveness research. This research has a strong 'equity focus and moral concern
to improve the quality of education for disadvantaged students' (Sammons
2007: 59).

The development of school effectiveness research over the last forty years
can be seen as a reaction to work in the USA by Jencks (1972) and Coleman
et al. (1966) who argued that the social class/prior achievement mix of schools
was the only school variable which seemed to have any impact on academic
outcomes (see Chapter 4 for more on this). This 'deterministic interpretation'
(Sammons et al. 1995: 2) of the factors related to academic achievement has
been countered by school effectiveness researchers who argue that although
background factors are important, it is schools that have the most significant
effect on student achievement and that this effect can be most pertinent for
young people from educationally disadvantaged backgrounds.

Two classic works on school effectiveness in the UK are Peter Mortimore
and colleagues' 1988 study of primary school life *School Matters* and the work
in secondary schools by Michael Rutter and colleagues (1979) called *Fifteen
Thousand Hours: Secondary Schools and Their Effects on Children* (the 15,000
hours is meant to denote the length of time a child spends in compulsory
education in the UK). Both books questioned why it was the case that some
schools appeared to be more 'effective' than others. The researchers' aim was
to tease out the effect of family background from the effect of the school and
to understand why in an effective school pupils were able to make better
progress than similar students who had attended a different school. From a
social justice perspective such work is particularly crucial and school effectiveness researchers argue that 'the life chances of students from socio-economically
disadvantaged backgrounds in particular are enhanced by effective schools,
those which foster both cognitive progress and promote social and affective
outcomes including and nation, self-esteem and student involvement
(Sammons 2007: 59).

What makes an effective school and teacher is a complex and difficult question to answer. Mortimore (1991: 14), for example, defines an effective school
as one in which 'students progress further than might be expected from a
consideration of its intake' and where pupils will exceed any expectations
made on the basis of the school's characteristics. In her recent review of

school effectiveness research, Sammons (2007) offers a number of general characteristics of effective schools:

- strong leadership;
- effective teaching;
- strong focus on learning;
- high and appropriate expectations for all;
- emphasis on rights and responsibilities;
- strong monitoring processes;
- ongoing professional development opportunities;
- productive involvement of parents.

Ineffective schools, on the other hand, are characterised by lack of vision, dysfunctional staff relationships and poor leadership, low-quality staff–pupil interactions, low expectations and inconsistent approaches to teaching and learning.

On the other hand, research into school effectiveness and school improvement is not without controversy. Rob Coe (2009: 363) argues, for example, that 'school improvement is much sought and often claimed'. Two criticisms often made of the field is that it is overly concerned with academic outcomes and that it downplays the important role that background factors play as determinants of educational success (see Chapter 4 for a further discussion on this). Gorard (2010: 745), for example, describes a number of ways in which schools could be considered 'effective'. They might have high levels of pupil attendance, pupil enjoyment of education, future pupil participation in education, pupil aspiration, preparation for citizenship, financial efficiency and so on. Another indicator of school success might be pupil scores in assessments intended to discover how much or how well they have learnt what is taught in school. And it is, of course, this final indicator of effectiveness that dominates, especially in school effectiveness research. But focusing on this one measure of school 'effectiveness' not only leads to a 'narrow understanding of what education is for', it also sidelines the importance of the relationship between pupil prior attainment and background that explains the vast majority of variation in school outcomes (Gorard 2010).

If we rank schools according to how well they perform in assessments such as the GCSE then we find that it is the schools which are located in affluent residential areas, which select their pupils on ability, wealth or possibly even religion, that are at the top of our league table. It is the schools that are located in less affluent areas, often inner cities, with high levels of pupil poverty and pupil mobility that will overwhelmingly appear at the bottom of the league table. This was true when Jencks (1972) and Coleman et al. (1966) did their ground breaking work in the USA in the late 1960s and it is also true today.

Any national or international league table of school performance will show that schools that teach the most disadvantaged students, in terms of their educational and socioeconomic background, will generally perform the least well on these tests. To what extent can this be seen as a 'failure' of schools to provide the best quality education for their pupils? If you subscribe to the view of school effectiveness researchers then these schools can and should improve. For although these researchers accept the important role that social characteristics play in educational success, they also argue that effective schools can overcome this disadvantage. However, if you subscribe to the second view and tend to side with Gorard that 'the whole school effectiveness model, as currently imagined, should be abandoned' (2010: 760) then you might argue that any apparent 'failure' is not the fault of the school but is instead more of a reflection on the characteristics of their intake. This would therefore suggest that current models of schools accountability which hold schools and teachers accountable for the academic attainment of their pupils are unreasonable. So how might an otherwise 'failing' school be turned into a successful one?

So far in this chapter we have just focused on school outcomes and accountability in the UK. However, it would be remiss to think that this is the only country where tests and sanctions have a key role to play in directing school reform policy. The next short section introduces an American perspective into the 'good' school debate.

Failing Schools? Perspectives from the USA

It is important to remember that dissatisfaction with national school systems do not just occur in the UK. Most of our economic competitor nations have their own 'crisis accounts' of falling standards and failing students and have initiated their own educational reforms that they hope will address them. This short section introduces the current path of reform in the USA. Dissatisfaction with American performance in both domestic and international assessments came to the fore in 1983 when President Ronald Regan's administration published the document *A Nation at Risk?* (NCEE 1983). This searing indictment of educational standards in the US signalled a shift in focus towards accountability and testing. The invective used in this document is strong and condemns the 'rising tide of mediocrity' eroding the American public school system:

> If an unfriendly foreign power had attempted to impose on America the mediocre educational performance that exists today, we might well have viewed it as an act of war. (NCEE 1983: 3)

The rhetoric is little different today. American students still occupy a mid-table position in the international achievement rankings and commentators and politicians still despair over the apparent underachievement of American schools:

> We have a genuine national crisis. More and more, we are divided into two nations. One that reads and one that doesn't. One that dreams and one that doesn't. (George Bush, Department of Education 2002)

Systems of high-stakes testing, epitomised by the 'No Child Left Behind' (NCLB) Act, have been put in place in order to raise standards in schools and to help propel the United States up the international school league tables. Under NCLB all schools and school districts receiving government funding are required to set targets and monitor progress in order to ensure that all students reach minimum levels of proficiency in English, Maths and Science. Failure to achieve these targets would lead to 'corrective action', which at its most extreme would result in school closure. Unlike the UK and many other industrialised countries, the United States has a very decentralised system of education, with much of the control over the day-to-day running of schools left in the hands of school districts acting on behalf of the individual states. There is no national system of assessment or a national curriculum; the responsibility for ascertaining standards, assessment tools and curriculum coverage lies with each state.

Arguably NCLB is very equitable in its intent: as its very title suggests, it demands that the academic progress of every child, regardless how able, be open to scrutiny. The concern among many commentators is that by forcing school improvement through sanctions linked to testing, many otherwise successful schools – in particular those which serve students in disadvantaged communities – may be unfairly labelled as failing (see Smith 2005a; West and Peterson 2003). These schools, which may serve communities with very transient populations, as well as teaching large proportions of students who have limited proficiency to speak English, are perhaps more likely to fail to secure the rigorous minimum competency levels demanded by the NCLB tests. As a consequence, such schools are likely to face sanctions such as the transfer of pupils from the school, reductions in school finance and, ultimately, school closure (Lee 2002; Sunderman 2008). Further unintended consequences of 'high-stakes tests' like NCLB have also drawn criticism; these include a narrowing of the curriculum, accusations of teachers 'teaching to the test' and an overemphasis on low-level skills (see Darling-Hammond 2007).

If you are interested in reading more about education in the United States then a good place to start is Spring (2011).

Inequalities in School Funding

In this final section we return to examine inequalities between different schools in the UK with a quick look into school funding. According to the OECD (2011b), schooling outcomes in the UK are among the most unequal of all member countries. This is partly due to 'a complex, multi-layered and poorly functioning deprivation funding system' (p. 93) in which government funds to support disadvantaged students are low by OECD standards and are often only partially spent on disadvantaged schools and students. Inequalities in school funding are particularly extreme in the USA, where money for schools is tightly linked to local house prices. So more affluent areas where the value of houses is higher attract greater funds for schools as they generate more money through property taxes. The same, of course, is not true in less affluent areas where houses are not worth as much. A fascinating account of the consequences of unequal school funding is provided by Jonathan Kozol (1991 and 2005).

In the UK state schools are mainly funded from the central government's education budget. Traditionally this money was then given to local authorities to distribute among the schools and other educational services in their area. However, in recent years the role of local authorities in allocating school funds has been gradually eroded as schools have become increasingly more autonomous in deciding how to spend their budgets (Sibieta et al. 2008). Funding for schools does vary according to the characteristics of their pupils. Schools with relatively large numbers of pupils from economically disadvantaged backgrounds (as measured by their eligibility to receive free school meals), or with pupils who have special educational needs also receive more funding. Indeed according to Sibieta et al. (2008: 34), pupils who are eligible for FSM 'attract over 70% more income to the school than pupils who are not eligible for FSM'.

So should schools be funded equally? If you were to adhere to the principle of *justice as equality* then you might argue that they should. However, there might be other arguments for funding schools with high levels of disadvantaged students at higher rates that could be based on principles of *need*. For example, students from disadvantaged communities might be more likely to have additional needs that require more funding, such as extra tutoring or the provision of breakfast clubs. Students with special educational needs might require additional teachers, resources and facilities. Data for school expenditure for 2009/10, however, reveals quite startling differences in the amount of funding that local authorities, and indeed the schools themselves, spend on their pupils. For example, the difference between the highest and lowest spending local authorities is around £4,000 per student. The gaps between individual schools are even greater.

Table 3.2 lists the eight secondary schools in England that spent the highest and lowest amounts of money on students in 2009/10. The gap separating these two groups of schools is quite staggering: over £16,000 per student. Think of how this gap would multiply over a class of 30 and then think of it across an entire school! There appears to be little difference in the characteristics of the schools in terms of GCSE attainment and the proportions eligible for FSM, although five of the lowest-funded schools do have very high proportions of FSM eligibility. However, it is important to note that the schools that receive the highest per student funding are also the smallest. Similarly these figures are only for the extreme groups (although median figures are also published in Table 3.2) and so might hide patterns that would be evident if you looked across more schools. If you are interested in doing this then there is a link to this dataset on the website that accompanies this book.

Table 3.2 Secondary school expenditure per pupil according to selected school characteristics, England 2009/10

School name	Number of pupils	Spending/pupil (£)	% 5+ A*–C GCSE (inc. Maths & Eng)	% FSM
Oak Farm Community School	138	18,131.88	27	29
Croxteth Community School	182	17,109.46	33	57
Skinners' Company's Girls School	308	13,976.99	39	45
Longton High School	244	13,312.20	40	23
Heywood Community High School	223	12,351.62	67	35
Furtherwick Park School	247	12,251.12	29	18
Deincourt Community School	322	11,876.39	40	15
Riverside Business and Enterprise College	415	11,873.78	30	29
Median for all English schools	1,000	5,212.35	55	11
Blessed Edward Oldcorne College	1,054	3,906.71	75	5.9
St Ambrose College	945	3,857.85	95	1.9
St Michael's CoE High School	1,135	3,816.30	79	3.5
Carlton Community College	1153	3,661.26	27	24
Knowsley Park Centre for Learning	1,252	3,652.24	36	30
Huyton Arts & Sports C for L	1,307	3,580.20	30	40
St Edmund Arrowsmith Catholic	886	1,551.11	55	24
All Saints Catholic C for L	1,161	1,529.81	38	33

Source: DfE (2011d).

 Reflection

In the commentary on Table 3.2 it was noted that the schools that appear to attract the highest per student spending are also the smallest. Why do you think that this might the case?

Summary

Despite the rhetoric around good schools for all students, schools can be unequal places for the pupils who attend them. One way in which the success of schools is increasingly being judged is by a country's performance in international tests of student achievement. These tests are very powerful in informing policy-makers and the public about the state of a country's schools. Indeed, PISA has become '*the* major international tool mobilising interest and debate on the relation of education with the knowledge economy agenda'

(Grek 2008: 4). The relatively poor performance of British schools in these tests, coupled with an ongoing dissatisfaction with the domestic school system, has led to different generations of policy-makers seeking new ways to improve schools. Current school improvement policies are characterised by increased choice for parents over the schools their children attend and a greater diversity in the sort of schools that are available. This is exemplified in particular by the current academy and free school movement in England. The impact of these policies on the attainment of pupils and on their enjoyment of school is uncertain but schools in Britain continue to be segregated. This, of course, has important implications for schools as fair and equitable institutions.

Further reading

'The future of comprehensive education': in this issue of the journal *Forum*, Tim Brighouse, former Director of Education of Birmingham City Council, and Clyde Chitty, Professor of Education, debate the future of the comprehensive school system. The full text of the debate is reproduced in *Forum*, 2003, 45 (1).

Gillard, D. (2010) 'Hobson's choice: education policies in the 2010 General Election', *Forum*, 52 (2): 135–44. This article provides a useful summary of education policy directly after the 2010 election, plus the author's own observations on the future for state education.

Two other books that focus on current education policy and school reform are:

Ball, S. (2008) *The Education Debate: Policy and Politics in the Twenty-First Century*. Bristol: Policy Press.

Fitz, J., Davies, B. and Evans, J. (2006) *Educational Policy and Social Reproduction: Class Inscription and Symbolic Culture*. Abingdon: Routledge.

Falling standards and failing students? Inequalities in student outcomes

Today, 'underachievement' is a synonym for much that is perceived to be wrong in today's society, from low scores in international children's reading tests to the social consequences of underachievement such as criminal behaviour, social exclusion and unsuccessful relationships and marriages. It is also a phenomenon which troubles our politicians, as this quotation from the former Secretary of Education shows:

> We face a genuine problem of underachievement among boys, particularly those from working-class families. This underachievement is linked to a laddish culture which in many areas has grown out of deprivation, and a lack of both self-confidence and opportunity.
>
> (David Blunkett, August 2000)

In addition the increased scrutiny of examination performance as the most tangible outcome of schooling has led to sections of the school population being labelled as failing or 'underachieving'. As we saw in Chapter 3 sophisticated international comparative tests such as PISA enable nations to look critically at the achievement of their students in the international arena. This has led to many countries re-examining their education systems in light of perceived failings in these comparative assessments. The consequence of this has frequently been dissatisfaction with the domestic school system, accusations of 'underachievement' and a 'crisis account' of falling academic standards. In this chapter we will look more closely at inequalities in the attainment of children and young people in school. While tests scores are not the only outcome of schooling, they are the ones which are subject to the most scrutiny and they also can have a profound impact on the lives of pupils as well as on the schools they attend.

Falling Standards and Failing Students

In the UK recent government policy has its focus firmly on raising standards and eliminating all forms of 'underachievement' in school (but see Box 4.1 for a discussion about the misuse of the term underachievement). One consequence of this attention is that we have a system of national testing and target setting that is of unprecedented scale. Within this discourse of falling standards and failing students sit concerns about the apparent failure of large sections of the school population. There will be few readers who have not heard of the 'underachieving boys' crisis, for example (see Epstein et al. 1998; Francis and Skelton 2005; DfES 2007; Smith 2003). However, educators also raise concerns about the relative attainment of some young people from certain ethnic minority groups (for example, Gillborn 2008) and those who come from the least wealthy homes (for example, Gorard 2000; Smith 2005b). Here we will examine inequalities in the academic attainment of each of these three groups in turn.

Gender Inequalities in Academic Attainment

Boys underachieving at school, says study. (Daily Telegraph, 14 August 2007)

As the above newspaper headline demonstrates the 'underachievement' of boys has received wide coverage in the media and elsewere. Indeed, evidence

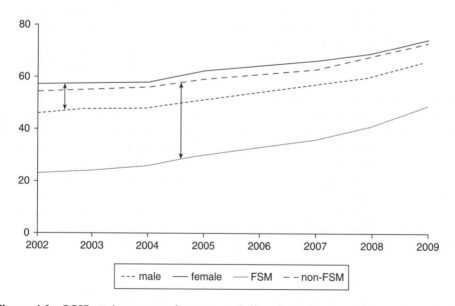

Figure 4.1   GCSE attainment gap between male/female students and those who are/not eligible for FSM

for the differential attainment of the nation's boys is not hard to find and it is easy to see why we might be concerned. For example, examination results, especially at GCSE, indicate that the performance of girls is higher than that of boys. The graph in Figure 4.1 shows the proportions of students who achieved five or more GCSE passes at grades A*–C between 2002 and 2009. As you can see, the performance of boys is consistently lower than that of girls. However, notice also that the scores of both boys and girls have risen throughout the past decade and that any differences in achievement between male and female pupils are dwarfed by the gaps between pupils who are eligible for free school meals and those who are not (a point we will return to later).

Despite the trends in Figure 4.1, comparatively little attention has been paid to recent improvements in the achievement levels of girls and the fact that the attainment of all pupils has risen steadily over the last 30 years is barely mentioned unless it is to raise concerns over falling standards and a 'dumbing down' of the school curriculum. In short, boys have fallen behind in this one crude measure of success and the dominant view is that something has to be done about it. Numerous feminist researchers have drawn attention to this 'backlash' (see, for example, Francis and Skelton 2005) and have made it clear that any attempts to raise the achievement of boys must not lose sight of the work done over the last three decades to improve the lot of girls in school. Several explanations for the apparent 'underachievement' of boys exist, three of the most widely used of which are summarised here.

Changing Masculinities

It has been argued that there are innate, natural-born differences between the sexes: boys are more likely to suffer from oxygen starvation at birth, they have poorer verbal reasoning skills, they mature later than girls, their parents do not talk to them as much as they do to their sisters and so on (Cohen 1998). However, according to some authors, these theories are based on 'crude versions of cognitive psychology' and have little basis in published research (Raphael Reed, 1998: 61). Mahony (1998: 42) links much of the 'hysteria' surrounding the underachieving youth or 'public burden number 1' to a fear among the male elite that men will lose ground to women in the workforce. The collapse in the postwar boom of heavy industry and the replacement (particularly in some working-class homes) of the male as the main family breadwinner, has led to what some researchers would call a change in the gender regime of these communities and another explanation for the poor performance of young men in our schools (Connell 1994).

The Classroom, the Teacher, Teaching and Learning

Claims about the feminisation of the school curriculum have come hand-in-hand with criticisms of female teachers for imposing female values on our pupils. Despite an uncertain evidence base, these claims are reworked as an explanation for the relatively poor performance of boys and in calls for an increase in the number of male teachers in our schools (but see Skelton et al. 2009b). The different behaviour and learning cultures of boys and girls is well documented (see, for example, Younger et al. 2005). In the classroom it is the boys who command the 'lion's share' of the teacher's attention and receive a disproportionate amount of the teacher's time compared with the girls. Boys can bring another agenda into the classroom, asserting themselves as jokers and as risk-takers, with a noisy approach to their work and a dislike of the tedium of writing. As a result, they are frequently the focus of classroom activity, whereas the girls are 'marginalised' on the edges (Francis 2000).

Assessment and the School Curriculum

Achievement gaps between boys and girls in English and other language- and literacy-based examinations is one key piece of evidence supporting the claim that boys are underachieving. The acquisition of literacy skills is important but is one that can sometimes be seen as a highly gendered activity. For example, research tells us that throughout school, girls are the keener readers who are more likely to be 'devoted' to their books (Millard 1997). When boys do read, their favoured genres – action and adventure and non-fiction – can leave them disadvantaged in the school curriculum, where narrative accounts that emphasise personal responses are favoured. However, although the English curriculum may well disadvantage boys, there is little correlation between achievement in English examinations and success in later life (Millard 1997), but as success in English examinations can act as a gatekeeper to education and employment opportunities, the disadvantage that boys have in acquiring the 'right' literacy skills can be compounded (see also DCSF 2009).

Thus there are three dominant explanations for the apparent 'under-achievement' of boys in schools: the conflict of masculinity in contemporary society, the curriculum and its assessment, and finally the everyday experience of both students and teachers within the classroom. In response to concerns about male underachievement, a plethora of strategies and initiatives have emerged. These range from experiments with single-sex teaching to networks of sports clubs aimed at encouraging 'failing' students to do better in school. However, the absence of rigorous trialling means that the efficacy of many of these strategies remains largely unproven. This is an important issue for educational research. Many of the initiatives that are used to try to improve pupil performance are poorly tested and the evidence as to whether they work can often be unclear (Coe 2009). If you are interested in reading more about the debates into 'what works' to improve education standards then Robert Slavin's accessible article is a good place to start (see Further reading at the end of the chapter).

Box 4.1 What do we mean by underachievement?

If you were to make a list of the issues that concern those who teach, research or seek to change the field of education, it would not be long before you came to 'underachievement'. In the UK in particular, the underachievement of boys is central to current 'crisis accounts' about falling standards and failing pupils. 'Underachievement' is a familiar word to those who work with young people; however, the term itself is not unproblematic. For example, how do you define underachievement and how do you measure it? Simply labelling one group of students, such as boys, as underachieving compared to another group, such as girls, tells us nothing about which boys may be in need of additional support in school and nothing about what the nature of this support might be. Ask yourself what any underachievement might be relative to and you will see how confusing the term is. Is it related to some kind of innate ability on the part of the individual or is it achievement relative to that of a larger group? In addition, the underachievement label is not only confined to describing the relative achievement of groups of students, or indeed individual students, it is frequently offered as an explanation for the relatively poorer academic performance of schools and of nations (Smith 2005b).

This conflation of 'underachievement' and 'low achievement' is important: underachievement and low achievement are not the same thing. Consider, for example, the student who, despite their best and most sustained efforts, fails to reach minimum proficiency levels on a given assessment. In the current climate of high-stakes testing, this individual might arguably be labelled a 'low achiever' but, given their hard work and sustained effort, is surely not an 'underachiever'. Consider another student, whose past achievement has suggested them to be academically very capable but whose relative lack of interest or effort has secured them a B grade rather than a top-scoring A grade. Arguably this individual is 'underachieving' but is surely not a 'low achiever'.

Thus anyone could underachieve at a given point in their school career, whether they are a 'gifted and talented' student, a new arrival to the school, male or of an ethnic minority. Arguably perhaps, underachievement is an individual phenomenon: a behaviour rather than an outcome. Of course this makes it a lot more difficult for schools to identify potential underachievement and to intervene, but underachievement is a complex phenomenon which can manifest itself in a range of behaviours and consequences for the individual. Underachievement is itself a concept over which there is much confusion and little consensus. In short, it is a term that has probably outlived its usefulness.

'Myths' about Boys' Underachievement

Given the complexity of the gender debate and uncertainties over what it is that we actually mean by the term underachievement, it is not surprising that an alternative account of the underachievement phenomenon also exists (Smith 2005b and see Box 4.1). For example, Sara Delamont (1999: 13) contends that 'it is pointless to be swept away by a moral panic about "failing", anti-school working-class boys. This is not a new problem.' Schools, she argues, have never been able to deal with the working-class boy. She goes on to argue that the whole standards debate is surrounded in a 'discourse of derision', compounded by a lack of understanding of the academic gains made by all pupils, and coupled with the media's resistance to hearing good news (Delamont 1999: 3). That 'underachievement' is not a new phenomenon has also been demonstrated in a historical study by Cohen (1998). She noted the seventeenth-century academic John Locke's consternation that young men found it difficult to succeed in Latin, while their younger sisters would 'prattle' on in French having had little or no formal instruction. The standard of the young men's English also gave him little joy. A more contemporary overview of the apparent myths surrounding boys' underachievement is provided by Skelton et al. (2009b). A few are summarised in Box 4.2.

Box 4.2

Myth: All boys underachieve and all girls now achieve well at school.

Reality: Many boys achieve highly and conversely many girls underperform.

Analysis of the attainment data shows that other factors or a combination of factors, such as ethnicity and social class, have a greater bearing on educational achievement than gender considered on its own (Skelton et al. 2009b: 3).

Myth: Changing or designing the curriculum to be 'boy-friendly' will increase boys' motivation and aid their achievement.

Reality: Designing a 'boy-friendly' curriculum has not been shown to improve boys' achievement.

There is no evidence to show that where schools have designed or changed parts of their curriculum to be more appealing to boys ('boy-friendly') it improves boys' achievement. Such changes may involve gender-stereotyping that can lead teachers to ignore pupils' actual preferences and limit the choices that either boys or girls can make (Skelton et al. 2009b: 6).

Myth: Boys underachieve across the curriculum.

Reality: Boys broadly match girls in achievement at maths and science.

Boys outperform girls in Maths at Key Stage 2 but there is a large gender gap favouring girls in English. This pattern is broadly reflected across OECD nations (see Table 4.1), and is of long standing. In the 1950s and 1960s it was commonplace to explain this difference in terms of boys' late development in language and literacy skills. Such relatively poor performance was not expected to hinder their educational progress over the long term (Skelton et al. 2009b: 3).

An International Perspective on Male and Female Attainment

As we saw in Chapter 3, the results from international comparative tests have an important role to play in influencing education policy at the national level. However, they are also useful in helping us understand the extent to which differences or inequalities in students' academic achievement are replicated across different nations. This might help us better understand the issues in our own country and may also help provide remedies. Table 4.1 compares student attainment in the Literacy assessment of the latest wave of PISA. As you can see, girls are performing consistently higher than boys in this test, even in countries with large differences in overall attainment such as Brazil and Finland. This is a trend that is replicated not only across all components of the PISA Literacy tests but across all countries participating in PISA 2009. However, not only are boys less likely to perform as well as girls in literacy assessments, they are also much less likely to say that they enjoy reading and consequently read for pleasure – again this hardly differs across all the countries that were involved in PISA 2009 (OECD 2010b, 2010c). The same patterns appear in the reading enjoyment and achievement of younger children who participation in PIRLS 2006 (Mullis et al. 2007).

You can see similar stable patterns in boy/girl attainment in literacy assessments if you were also to track progress over time as well as across different

Table 4.1 Student performance on PISA reading assessment (reflect and evaluate subscale) according to sex

Country	Mean score (boys)	Mean score (girls)
Australia	501	543
Brazil	408	437
Canada	516	555
Finland	506	565
France	472	517
Germany	470	513
Japan	498	545
Korea	521	565
Mexico	419	445
United Kingdom	489	516
United States	498	527

Source: OECD (2010b).

countries (Smith 2010). So, notwithstanding the technical and conceptual problems of comparing test data across different years, cohorts and nations (for example, Newton 2005; Prais 2003), it does appear that achievement gaps between male and female students in literacy-based subjects are relatively well established across time, as well as appearing resistant to various cultural and educational settings. This constancy might make us reconsider some of the explanations given for the apparent underachievement (or perhaps differential attainment might be a better term) of boys in literacy-based assessments.

Ethnic Group Inequalities in Academic Attainment

For almost half a century, there has been concern over the relatively poor attainment in school examinations of students from some ethnic minority[1] backgrounds. Attention has tended to focus on the attainment of students of Caribbean origin, who were not only being outperformed in the curriculum but were also more likely to be excluded from school. Explanations for these differences have tended to focus on home background factors, language and culture, as well as low teacher expectations (Tomlinson 1987). Concern about attainment gaps and high rates of school exclusion among some ethnic groups have continued, with recent research suggesting that despite higher levels of attainment by all young people, there are increasing gaps in the academic achievement of some ethnic minority groups (Gillborn 2008; Strand 2011). Figure 4.2 shows rather crudely the attainment gap at

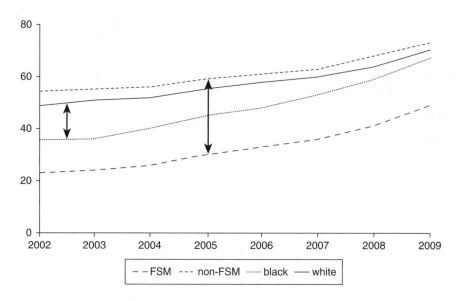

Figure 4.2   Attainment gap between black/white students, compared with FSM eligibility

GCSE between students loosely termed as black and white. White students continue to achieve at higher levels than black students but the gap is closing and does still remain smaller than the FSM gap.

Explanations for the Attainment Gap

One explanation for the relatively lower attainment of students from some ethnic minority groups is that they tend to come from poorer homes. For example, two-fifths of people from ethnic minorities live in low-income households, twice the rate of white people. This is particularly high for Bangladeshi and Pakistani families, of whom around 70 per cent and 60 per cent respectively live in the poorest households (Poverty Site 2010d; see also Kenway and Palmer 2007). However, recent work by Strand (2011) suggests that differences in attainment, particularly between White British and Black Caribbean and Black African groups cannot always be explained by socioeconomic status. Strand suggests that there are other explanations besides poverty that we need to consider when trying to explain achievement gaps between minority ethnic groups; these might include teacher expectations, racism and cultural differences. Indeed, the role that schools and teachers play in reinforcing racial stereotypes and in failing to tackle the low attainment of students from some minority ethnic backgrounds has concerned researchers for some time. David Gillborn and Mairtin Mac an Ghaill have written extensively on ethnic minority inequalities in school – see the references to their work in the Further reading at the end of the chapter.

In trying to explain the reasons for the disenchantment of some ethnic minority pupils with the education system, Gillborn and Youdell (2000) point to several factors inherent in what they see as the 'A–C economy' of schools which specifically disadvantages pupils from some minority groups. They claim that in order to preserve a high league table position, schools use selection, ability testing and streaming as a way of maximising the number of pupils who pass the all-important five or more A*–C GCSE grade threshold. In doing so, the authors claim that schools are not providing all pupils with equal access to the curriculum, because in some cases pupils are being encouraged to sit fewer GCSE examinations. These findings are similar to those from earlier studies of multi-ethnic inner-city schools conducted in the mid-to-late 1980s (Mac an Ghaill 1988; Gillborn 1990). These authors seek to highlight the injustices of the education system for pupils from minority backgrounds.

This section has given a very brief overview of patterns of educational inequalities among ethnic minority groups in Britain. To provide an international perspective on ethnic minority attainment we will briefly consider educational inequalities between ethnic groups in the USA. Although the cultural and historical context surrounding ethnic inequalities are different in the US than in the UK, this will nevertheless provide a useful illustration of how inequalities persist across different educational systems.

Racial Inequalities in American Schools

In 1892, a young man named Homer Plessy boarded a train travelling from New Orleans to Covington, Louisiana. He took his seat in a compartment which was designated as 'whites only'. Homer Plessy was one eighth Negro and of fair complexion. He was told to leave the carriage and sit in the 'coloured' area of the train. He refused and was arrested.

Almost thirty years before Homer Plessy took the train to Covington the American Civil War had ended. In the period of reconstruction which followed, all slaves were freed and were given the right to vote. So began a period of political struggle in the American South between the rights of the freed slaves to be treated as full citizens and the resistance this encountered from many whites. In 1868, three years after the Civil War had ended, the Fourteenth Amendment to the US Constitution provided for equality for black Americans. In a clause which stated that 'No state shall ... deny to any person within its jurisdiction the equal protection of laws', it mandated that equal laws would apply to everyone, freed slaves included. Later the US Supreme Court ruled that this 'equal protection' could also mean 'separate but equal'. This ruling is important as it led, in many parts of the South, to the legally sanctioned separation of whites and blacks (and other non-white groups) in all public facilities. Also known as the Jim Crow laws, this segregation meant separate transport, cinemas, restaurants and restrooms. For students this meant separate classroom, schools and universities. The Jim Crow laws remained in place until 1954 when the legal challenge brought about by *Brown* v. *Board of Education of Topeka* overturned the separate but equal doctrine and argued that segregated education was illegal on the basis that even if school facilities were identical in two racially segregated schools (and often they were not), the schools would be deemed unequal because they were racially segregated. Thus began a period of racial desegregation which, led by Martin Luther King and the Civil Rights movement, spread beyond schooling to other aspects of life. Desegregating the South's schools was, however, not without protest and in many places was characterised by vocal and violent protests such as those at Little Rock High School in Arkansas in 1957 where white citizens objected violently to the integration of nine black students. The Civil Rights Act which was passed by Congress in 1964 did speed up the process of school desegregation as well as introducing legislation which withheld federal funds for school districts that practised racial desegregation.

Although *Brown* v. *Board of Education* mandated equal access to education for black students, inequalities in their educational experience, as well as those of young people from Hispanic and, in particular, Native-American backgrounds, still persist. For example, young people from

African-American backgrounds have higher instances of school dropout, and juvenile criminality, coupled with lower levels of university and college entrance (Darling-Hammond 2007; Frankenberg et al. 2010). In addition, research by the Civil Rights Project based at UCLA also shows that rather than encouraging schools to become better integrated, recent accountability policies, such as No Child Left Behind (see Chapter 3), are in fact moving schools towards greater inequalities and increased levels of segregation (Sunderman 2008; Saporito and Sahoni 2006; Kozol 2005).

The National Assessment of Educational Progress (NAEP) is a large-scale national test that is used to monitor achievement trends in the United States. Also known as the 'Nation's Report Card', NAEP has been undertaking nation-wide annual assessments of student achievement in various subjects since 1969. In addition, the NAEP long-term trends assessment has been administering the same set of tests to 9, 13 and 17 year olds since 1971 in reading and since 1973 in mathematics, so making it possible to track educational progress over extended periods of time (NCES 2009). Figure 4.3 shows the trends in average reading scores for 13-year-old students between 1971 and 2008. The same pattern in black/white attainment in reading occurs here as in national examinations at 16 in England and Wales, and reflects an achievement gap in favour of white students that appears to have existed over the last three decades.

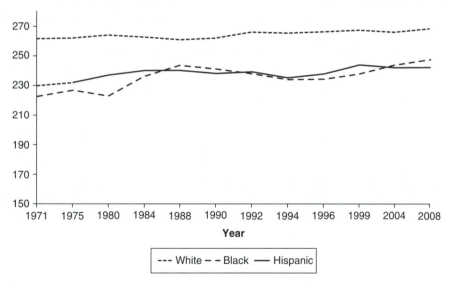

Figure 4.3 Average reading scores among 13-year-old students according to ethnic group
Source: NCES (2009).

In the following section, we turn to our third group and examine inequalities in educational attainment according to socioeconomic group.

Educational Inequalities According to Socioeconomic Group

> Rich thick kids do better than poor clever children. (Michael Gove, Secretary of State for Education, July 2010)

As Michael Gove puts it rather crudely in the above quotation, social class and education are 'inextricably linked' (Davison 2010: 69; also Gorard 2000; Hirsch 2007). Indeed, you can see from Figures 4.1 and 4.2 above that differences in attainment in national tests are much wider between those who are eligible for free school meals and those who are not (see also OECD 2011b). However, as an area of research, socioeconomic educational inequalities have become subsumed by a more recent focus on differential achievement according to gender and ethnicity (Strand 2011). Concern by mainly feminist researchers during the 1970s and 1980s into differential learning outcomes and educational opportunities for girls and the ensuing 'moral panics' of the 1990s sourrounding male underachievement, coupled with concern about the achievement and increasing exclusion rates and disaffection of students from ethnic minority communities, has sought to move research into the attainment of working-class students to the margins. Indeed, according to Davison, it has become 'unfashionable' to discuss education and social class: 'There appears to be an underlying assumption that it is now passé to do so: the debate has moved on; social class is an irrelevance' (2010: 61).

Perhaps this new emphasis is unsurprising – teachers can easily differentiate between the boys and girls in their class or between students from visible ethnic minority groups. With the current emphasis on raising standards, any differences in attainment or behaviour among these groups is much more visible and open to comment. It is a lot more difficult for teachers to identify the students in their classes who come from poorer homes, particularly in the secondary school where teachers might teach well over 120 students a day and be less familiar with an individual's home circumstances than a colleague in the primary sector. As a consequence, trends in the performance and learning behaviours and trajectories of this group of students might be a lot more difficult to determine, although a more cynical reason for the replacement of poverty as a key focus of educational comparisons may simply be that there is little schools or society can do (or indeed would seek to do) about whether one is born female or black. On the other hand, there are clear implications for social justice if academic success is seen to be dependent upon whether or not you come from a home where your parents have never worked.

Box 4.3 Free school meals and family poverty

Whether or not a child is eligible for free school meals is a widely used proxy for family income in educational research in the UK. In order to be eligible for free school meals a child has to be living in a household where parents receive income support, job seekers allowance or similar benefits. In official records, eligibility for free school meals is counted only if a child is both eligible and claiming free school meals (Hobbs and Vignoles 2010). This can be confusing because not all families who are eligible for free school meals will decide to take them. Some reasons why families might decide not to receive free school meals are discussed by Storey and Chamberlin (2001). Data published by the DCSF in 2008 show that nearly 12 per cent of pupils in England receive free school meals (DCSF 2008). However, around 30 per cent of English children live in households where no one works, meaning that there are nearly 1.4 million children who are entitled to free school meals but who do not claim them it. This suggests that very large numbers of the poorest children may be missing out.

Monitoring achievement according to socioeconomic status has both conceptual and practical difficulties. Schools rarely record the occupations of their students' parents; while free school meals, the most widely used proxy measure for family poverty, is an imperfect measure of socioeconomic status, not simply because it takes no account of families who do not take up their free meal entitlement (see Box 4.3). Many of the explanations for the relatively poor academic performance of students from poorer homes have focused on family background and composition factors, as well as on parental education levels and their involvement in their child's schooling (for example, Laureau 1987; Kiernan and Mensah 2011). Within the sociology of education there is a long and distinguished research literature on the role of social class in education and suggested reading is given at the end of this chapter. Such work is exemplified by research by Coleman et al. (1966) and Jencks (1972) in the USA which suggested that family background was the single most important contributor to success in school, an argument which has prompted a great deal of research focusing on the structural characteristics of families such as socioeconomic status (SES) and family make-up.

In addition to empirical work which has examined the relationship between family background and educational attainment there have been a number of academics who provide theoretical explanations for these inequalities (see Raffo et al. 2007 for a more theoretically focused account of the relationship between education and poverty). Possibly the most widely cited of these theorists is Pierre Bourdieu. There is not the space here to discuss Boudieu's work in detail, and there are many notable texts that can do this a lot better than I (see, for example, Ball 2004), but the basic thesis of his work is as follows.

Bourdieu argues that different social groups have different 'cultural capitals' (experiences, knowledge and connections) and that these cultural attributes are valued differently by society. Schooling acts to reproduce and reinforce certain cultural values and so students whose cultural capital fits that of the school are more likely to succeed (Bourdieu 1977). This fit may be apparent in aspects of the hidden curriculum, such as language, values and attitudes towards education, with which students with a certain cultural capital might be more familiar. Students whose cultural capital does not fit with the dominant culture of the school might be left at a disadvantage. Bourdieu illustrates this with the example of museum entry. Entry to museums is generally free of charge so there are no economic obstacles to attendance. However, it is mainly the middle classes who visit museums. In the same way, schools are largely middle-class institutions (teaching tends to be regarded as a middle-class profession after all) where middle-class children tend to fit in better and so are likely to be more successful.

The argument that social class and/or family background are the key determinants of educational success is a powerful one. However, what does this mean for those researchers, teachers or individuals who are interested in reducing educational inequalities? If schools make such little difference in raising the academic attainment of certain social groups, then other than making a difference at the individual level what realistically can we expect of our schools?

One consequence of recent education policies has been the gradual removal of schools from local government control and increased involvement of private individuals and organisations. This can be seen in free schools in England and the charter school movement in the USA, and is exemplified by the work of the former tennis player André Agassi in his home city of Las Vegas in the USA.

Raising The Aspirations and Attainment of Disadvantaged Students: An Example from America

The Andrè Agassi College Preparatory Academy (AAPCPA) is a tuition-free charter school located in Clark County school district, Las Vegas, Nevada, USA. As its name suggests, the school was founded by the tennis player André Agassi who writes in his autobiography that:

> ... I resolve to build the best Charter school in America ... to hire the best teachers, pay them well, and hold them accountable for grades and test scores. We resolve to show the world what can be done when you set standards outrageously high and open the purse strings. (Agassi 2009: 261)

The school opened in 2001 for students aged between 8 and 10 years old. It now teaches children from kindergarten (age 5 or 6) through to the end of high school. In 2009 every member of the graduating class had secured a place at college. The mission of the school is to be a

> centre of strength ... [to provide] an array of choices and opportunities to underserved communities. By harnessing the talents of gifted educational entrepreneurs, [the school] works to produce inspired, creative, ethical, compassionate, and reflective leaders who offer solutions to the problems posed by a democratic society. (p. 289)

The school is oversubscribed and places are allocated by lottery. It has high expectations of its students who are required to attend from 7.30 AM to 3.30 PM each day and, unusually for public schools in America, to wear a school uniform. It also has high expectations of its teachers. They are expected to follow a 'Commitment to Excellence' which requires them to undertake additional developmental courses where necessary, and also to make sure that every student and parent in their class has their home phone number in case they need to contact them out of school hours. Parental engagement is also highly prized and parents must commit to reading with their child each night, to checking their homework and to volunteering at the school. AACPA is housed in a new $40 million campus located in one of the most economically deprived parts of Las Vegas. As Agassi writes: 'Through a mix of state funding and private donors, we're going to invest heavily in kids and thereby prove that in education, as in all things, you get what you pay for' (2009: 336).

Such philanthropy and commitment is, of course, laudable and it is a model for schooling that the Coalition government seeks to emulate in the free school initiative in England that was described in Chapter 3. But is Agassi's school successful in terms of student achievement? As described earlier, all public schools in America are held accountable for student performance through the No Child Left Behind Act that requires schools to make Adequate Yearly Progress (AYP) in state-wide targets in English Language Arts and Mathematics. In both 2009 and 2010, AACPA made Adequate Yearly Progress in each of Nevada's NCLB targets (Nevada Department of Education 2010), so on that measure, yes it is a successful school. In fact only around one third of the 226 elementary schools in the Clark County School District made AYP in 2009/10. You can read more about the Andrè Agassi College Preparatory Academy at the school and its foundation's websites: http://www.agassiprep.org/ and http://www.agassifoundation.org/.

Let us look a little more closely at the characteristics of the students who attend André Agassi's school. Table 4.2 provides some background information on the students who attend the Elementary school section of AACPA and their attainment in NCLB assessments. It compares this with two other local schools which are not charter schools: Matt Kelly Elementary School, a school located a very short distance from AACPA, and Ann Lynch Elementary School, which is located about five miles away but has a somewhat different school population.

Table 4.2 Pupil background characteristics and academic attainment in three Nevada elementary schools

	AACPA	Kelly Elementary	Lynch Elementary
Limited English Proficiency (%)	0	18.7	63.7
Special Educational Needs (%)	10.6	22.2	10.2
Receiving FSM (%)	0	100	95.5
African-American students (%)	92	72.4	11.9
AYP in English Language Arts?	Yes	No	Yes
AYP in Mathematics?	Yes	No	Yes
Overall designation	Adequate	In need of improvement	Adequate

Source: Nevada Department of Education AYP results 2009–10.

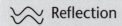

Reflection

What patterns can you discern from Table 4.2 in terms of the relationship between student characteristics and school attainment? What might they tell you about charter schools more broadly?

While this is just one example of one charter school in the United States, it does provide an insight to a very different concept of schooling to the traditional view of local public schools. The debate about whether increased school competition improves academic outcomes is hotly contested. But as we saw in Chapter 3 this is a model of school improvement that is favoured in the UK as well as the USA. The impact that this increased competition will have on the attainment and life chances of the young people who attend the schools will be closely monitored.

Summary

This chapter has examined inequalities in academic attainment that exist between different groups of students, namely according to sex, ethnic group and social class. The importance of ensuring a fair and equitable schooling experience for all students is implicit in many societies, and a consideration of current 'moral panics' surrounding the underachievement of different student groups provides a useful case study to help us consider what it is that we can reasonably expect from our schools and exactly which (if any) groups of young people are being let down by our education system. Perhaps it is inevitable that education systems that are so heavily focused on examination outcomes present such considerable inequalities for certain individuals. But are these inequalities all unfair? Certain inequalities in the examination system seem to be acceptable: if some students achieve higher examination results than others then that is considered to be the natural outcome of exams. On the other hand, inequalities in the achievement of specific groups of students, for example boys and girls, are considered widely to be unjust. This chapter has only considered academic inequalities. Lest we forget, test scores are not the only outcomes of schooling. We consider these additional benefits of schooling in Chapter 6.

Reflection: Closing the achievement gap

In this book we have been thinking about how education might be distributed in order to make it fairer and improve social justice. We argued in Chapter 3 that funding schools equally might be unfair because certain groups of students, those with special educational needs for example, need additional funding in order to make their experiences of education more equitable. The meritocratic concept upon which our education system is based is also problematic. This seeks to reward attainment purely on merit (on talent or effort perhaps) and to seek to eliminate background disadvantage. But this will also require additional resources to be given to one group (the motivated and/or the talented) instead of another (those with less talent and/or motivation) (Brighouse and Swift 2008).

Another way of distributing education equally could be to ensure equality of outcome, for example in school examinations. This motivation can be seen behind strategies to close the achievement gap that we have seen in this chapter. However, given the role of social factors in educational attainment, this would also require that additional funds and other resources be given to the least advantaged and, of course, parents with the resources to do so can remove their children from the state school system and so gaps will persist.

- Does this mean then that educational equality, through outcome or even opportunity, is unattainable?
- If it is important that we do close the achievement gap, then where should we close it? Would it be fairest to reduce the gap between the highest and lowest performers, between the lowest and the middle, or to raise the performance of everyone but with a gap still in place?
- The scrutiny of examination data alongside the assumption that students should not underachieve in school because they are male, black or from the working class presents something of a paradox: what are examinations for if not to differentiate between groups of students? How would you answer this contention?

Note

1. The term 'minority ethnic' as used to describe these students is in itself problematic as it suggests a group that is 'marginalised' or 'less important'; it also implies a homogeneity that fails to recognise the huge diversity among these groups (Arora 2010).

Further reading

Epstein, D., Elwood, J., Hey, V. and Maw, J. (1998) *Failing Boys? Issues in Gender and Achievement*. Buckingham: Open University Press.

Francis, B. and Skelton, C. (2005) *Reassessing Gender and Achievement: Questioning Contemporary Key Debates*. Abingdon: Routledge.

Gillborn, D. (2008) *Racism and Education: Coincidence or Conspiracy?* London: Routledge.

Gorard, S. (2000) *Education and Social Justice*. Cardiff: University of Wales Press.

Mac an Ghaill, M. (1988) *Young, Gifted and Black*. Buckingham: Open University Press.

Slavin, R. E. (2002) 'Evidence-based education policies: transforming educational practice and research', *Educational Researcher*, 31 (7): 15–21.

Classic books that examine social inequalities in schooling include:

Douglas, J. W. B. (1945) *The Home and The School: A Study of Ability and Attainment in the Primary School*. London: Panther Modern Society.

Halsey, A. H., Heath, A. F. and Ridge, J. M. (1980) *Origins and Destinations: Family, Class and Education in Modern Britain*. Oxford: Clarendon Press.

Jackson, D. and Marsden, B. (1962) *Education and the Working Class*. London: Routledge & Kegan Paul.

For a US perspective, try:

Berliner, D. and Biddle, B. (1995) *The Manufactured Crisis: Myths, Fraud and the Attack on America's Public Schools*. Reading, MA: Addison-Wesley.

Kozol, J. (1991) *Savage Inequalities*. New York: Harper Perennial.

Kozol, J. (2005) *The Shame of the Nation*. New York: Three Rivers Press.

5

Included or excluded? Social justice and special educational needs

[There is a] fundamental contradiction within the education systems of the UK and USA between an intention to treat all learners as essentially the same and an equal and opposite intention to treat them as different.

(Dyson 2001: 5)

Some commentators frequently refer to educational issues as being cyclical and none more so perhaps than the 'inclusion' of children and young people with special educational needs (SEN) in mainstream schools. In this short chapter, we will look at some of the inequalities that are experienced by young people with special educational needs as well as some of the challenges in deciding where best they should be educated.

The recent Lamb Inquiry into Special Educational Needs and Parental Confidence considers that:

Children who have a learning difficulty or disability that requires additional support, more than is normally offered in a classroom, have SEN. (Lamb Inquiry 2009: 16)

In 2009, just under 3 per cent of all young people in school had a statement of special educational needs. A statement is a legal document which outlines what support a young person is entitled to and how it should be provided. Young people with statements tend to be those with the most need. In addition to statemented pupils, a further 18 per cent of those in school are identified as having special educational needs (DfE 2010f). This group of pupils will have their needs addressed largely by the school with limited involvement from outside agencies, such as the educational psychology service. Special educational needs can comprise a range of different conditions. They tend to be grouped into four categories: cognition and learning needs; behaviour, emotional and social development needs; communication and interaction needs; and finally sensory and/or physical needs (see Hodkinson and Vickerman 2009 for a detailed introduction to the area).

There are important differences in the characteristics of young people with special educational needs. For example, they are more likely to be male and to be eligible to receive free school meals while being less likely to be of Chinese or Asian ethnic origin. Around 1 per cent of the school population are educated in special schools, the vast majority (around 97 per cent) of whom have statements (DfE 2010f). Young people with special educational needs also experience significant inequalities in school: they are more likely to be excluded from school, suffer from episodes of bullying and have higher rates of absence and school refusal than their peers without SEN (Lamb Inquiry 2009). And when they leave school, they are also more likely to be NEET (not in employment, education and training) (DfE 2011e).

It was the 1978 Warnock Report on special education which laid the foundation of the principles by which young people with SEN are taught in schools today. The Report introduced the concept of special educational needs as a continuum of need and called for parents to be seen as partners, alongside professionals, in making decisions about the best provision for their child. Some years later Baroness Mary Warnock revisited the debate with a new critique of the current system of schooling for young people with SEN and disabilities (Warnock and Norwich 2010). The discussion that Mary Warnock's paper generated revealed much of the confusion and uncertainty around special educational needs that exist today, most notably in terms of the problems of categorising different types of need (Warnock and Norwich 2010), of purported over-identification of SEN (Maddern 2010), and of issues with the statementing process and the 'postcode lottery' surrounding identification and care (Ofsted 2010). Of all these issues, however, the topic of inclusion – teaching children with and without SEN side by side – is arguably among the most contentious.

Inclusion

The 1981 Education Act provided the impetus that enabled more young people with various forms of 'learning disabilities' to be taught in mainstream classrooms. Prior to the Warnock Report, children and young people identified as 'handicapped' or 'educationally subnormal' were taught in special schools or in 'remedial' units which might be located on the same site as the mainstream school (MacBeath et al. 2006). Such categorisation of pupils was also based upon a deficit model of need, emphasising what young people could *not*, rather than what they could, do. The labelling of individuals in this way was also considered to be both 'offensive' and 'inaccurate' and the 1981 Education Act banned the use of such terms and replaced them with 'special educational need'.

Since the 1981 Act there has been a steady movement towards the inclusion of all pupils in mainstream schools: inclusive education it seems 'is needed as a means to achieve social justice for students with disabilities' (Artiles et al. 2006). Such a commitment is enshrined in the UN Convention on the Rights of Persons with Disabilities (OHCHR 2006). Article 24 of the Convention states that:

- Persons with disabilities are not excluded from the general education system on the basis of disability, and that children with disabilities are not excluded from free and compulsory primary education, or from secondary education, on the basis of disability;
- Persons with disabilities can access an inclusive, quality and free primary education and secondary education on an equal basis with others in the communities in which they live.

The previous Labour government fully embraced the ideal of inclusion. Their 1997 White Paper *Excellence for All Children: Meeting Special Educational Needs* set out their intention to 'promote the inclusion of children with SEN within mainstream schooling wherever possible' (DfEE 1997: 5). The 2001 Special Education Needs and Disability Act further strengthened the rights of children with SEN to be educated in the mainstream (Hodkinson and Vickerman 2009).

However, the issue of 'inclusion' is arguably among most contentious in the field of SEN. It is one which sparks polarised debate between those who see inclusion as a human rights issue and advocate that all children with SEN are taught in mainstream schools (necessitating the closure of all special schools), and those who see inclusion policy as 'the root of all problems in SEN' (House of Commons Education and Skills Committee 2006: 22). Inclusion is a problematic term to define. One perspective views 'inclusion' in terms of where pupils are taught (in a mainstream or a special school, for instance). Another sees 'inclusion' in broader terms as concerning all learners, not only those with special educational needs: 'The aim of inclusion is to reduce exclusion and discriminatory attitudes, including those in relation to age, social class, ethnicity, religion, gender and attainment' (Ainscow et al. 2006: 2).

From a social justice perspective, advocates of inclusion argue that separating students on the basis of education need is no different to now-illegal minority group segregation practices. While 'opponents' of inclusion point to the limitations of the mainstream classroom and argue for the specialist support and instruction that is available to young people through specialised provision (Ferguson 2008). The situation we are presented with is paradoxical: on the one hand special schools offer support and pedagogical approaches that effectively address their students' needs, but on the other, these students are taught on the margins of their peers' society, a situation which may ill prepare them for life as fully integrated citizens. The role of inclusion is central to many contemporary debates around special education, as well as providing a thought-provoking exercise in deciding issues of fairness in how these young people are educated. Therefore the remainder of this chapter is devoted to an exposition of some of these differing perspectives. It is worthy of note, however, that at the time of writing the Coalition government had released a consultation Green Paper on Special Educational Needs and Disability (DfE 2010g). The following sentiment is writ large in this report:

There should be real choice for parents and that is why we are committed to removing any bias towards inclusion that obstructs parent choice and preventing the unnecessary closure of special schools. (p. 51)

Under these proposals, parents and other groups would be able to set up special free schools, particularly in areas where existing special schools are at risk of closure. The circle, it appears, is turning.

Contrasting Views on Inclusion

In this section we will consider two somewhat opposing views on inclusion. We begin with four short extracts which present the case for inclusion. This is then followed by a larger extract from Mary Warnock's recent pamphlet *Special Educational Needs: A New Look* (Warnock and Norwich 2010).

The case for inclusive education

Inclusion is not easy but it makes sense. Of course it would be much easier for teachers to separate children according to their abilities, their disabilities and their strengths and weaknesses. They could then fit into the little boxes we insist on forcing them into. Why not go the whole way and segregate them by race, by religion, by language and by social class? All our children need to be part of their community and to separate them out of that community in special schools is too simple. (Frederick 2005)

Our school system is the key place in our society where people from all backgrounds learn to live together. Inclusion is not just about a few children with learning, physical or behavioural impairments being 'placed' in mainstream schools. It is about creating a society where all people can find their own unique place and work together for the benefit of all. If this work is not started at school – then what hope do we have as a society? (Alliance for Inclusive Education, at:http://www.allfie.org.uk/pages/hfi.html)

Until very recently all children with any kind of 'special need' from a limp to severe learning difficulties were sent to special schools. We are living with the results. They may 'work' from the point of view of the non-disabled world which wants us out of sight, looked after by saints and causing no trouble to anyone, but they do not work from the point of view of human beings who want to be visible, accepted, to be valued, to have a role in society. (Extract taken from Micheline Mason's website: http://www.michelinemason.com/topics/inclusion.htm)

The existence of segregated 'special' schools stifles creativity of mainstream schools about how to respond to diversity and weakens their responsibilities to include all learners. It undermines efforts to develop inclusive education by draining resources from mainstream, which in turn sets back the development of inclusive communities. Segregated schooling appeases the human tendency to negatively label those perceived as different. It gives legal reinforcement and consolidation to a deeply embedded, self-fulfilling, social process of devaluing and distancing others on the basis of appearance and ability in order to consolidate a sense of normality and status. (CSIE 2003, cited in Thomas and Vaughan 2004: 111)

The case against inclusive education

The concept of inclusion springs from hearts in the right place. Its meaning, however, is far from clear, and in practice it often means that children are physically included but emotionally excluded. Inclusion should mean being involved in a common enterprise of learning, rather than being necessarily under the same roof.

In the context of education, we need to ask whether children who have special needs, that is children, who for various reasons have difficulties in learning at school, do in fact participate more in the enterprise of education if they are taught in mainstream schools than if they are taught in special schools. The answer, surely, is that some of them do, but some of them do not. As I have suggested already 'SEN children' increasingly tend to be lumped together indiscriminately, as though they share in common a right to be educated in mainstream schools. But the idea of 'learner-centered education', increasingly seen as important for educational success, should remind us that for some children participation is impossible in the context of the mainstream school.

Schools are for children, not adults; and children still need help in their development. Education is a unique enterprise in that it is necessarily a temporary phase of life, directed towards the future, towards life after school. The pursuit of equality at school may mean taking whatever steps are necessary now to ensure equal opportunities later on. It should not be thought to entail an insistence that all children within a given area should be literally in the same school. What is needed is that all children should be included within a common educational project, not that they should be included under one roof.

Inclusion is not a matter of where you are geographically, but of where you belong. There are many children, and especially adolescents, identified as having special educational needs, who can never feel that they belong in a large mainstream school. We must give up the idea that SEN is the name of a unified class of students at whom, in a uniform way, the policy of inclusion can be directed. That schools should as far as possible adapt their premises to make all parts of them more accessible to children in wheelchairs, or whose mobility is otherwise restricted is something that, though it may be expensive, is a policy that is easy to understand and in principle to implement. Special equipment may make it possible that some children with sensory deprivation or who cannot write or communicate without electronic aids can be taught in the ordinary classroom.

However, not every child who suffers from such disabilities as these will flourish in a mainstream school, however much the environment is adapted. Children with such disabilities are often vulnerable in other ways as well. (Mary Warnock, *Special Educational Needs: A New Look,* in Warnock and Norwich 2010: 32–5).

〰 Reflection

What are your views on these different arguments for and against educating all children, regardless of need, together?

〰 Reflection

In her article, Mary Warnock makes several assertions about the role of schooling which are worthy of further consideration. For example that:

- Schools are not a 'microcosm of society'; rather they are a temporary phase, a preparation for society and all that entails.
- In order to achieve equality of opportunity in later life outcomes, different treatments at the school level are entirely appropriate.
- Children do not need to be educated 'under one roof'.
- No matter what adaptations are made to the physical fabric of schools, some children and young people will never be able to flourish there.

Together these points make an interesting basis for a discussion about the purpose of schooling as a preparation for future life. They can perhaps best be summed by a question that Mary Warnock poses to Brahm Norwich's response to her paper:

Are children with special educational needs to be educated as if they were the same as their fellow pupils, or as if they were different, and different, too, from one another, each with individual needs that must be met if they are to flourish? (Warnock and Norwich 2010: 120)

Further reading

Hodkinson, A. and Vickerman, P. (2009) *Key Issues in Special Educational Needs and Inclusion.* London: Sage.

Slee, R. (2011) *The Irregular School: Exclusion, Schooling and Inclusive Education.* London: Routledge.

Warnock, M. and Norwich, B. (2010) *Special Educational Needs: A New Look,* ed. L. Terzi. London: Continuum.

Pupils' experiences of social justice in school

A key purpose of education is to increase participation and achievement among school pupils, especially those facing disadvantage in terms of language, poverty, ability and special needs. This is something that we take for granted. Another purpose is to enhance pupils' enjoyment of learning and their preparation for citizenship. As we have seen in Chapters 3 and 4, most discussion around educational issues tends to concern achievement. Far less attention has been put into considering how to promote experiences of fairness, enjoyment and 'good' citizenship, and how to recognise success or failure in this (see Osler 2010). For many pupils, what happens to them at school is fundamental to their conception of wider society and their sense of what is just and fair (Gorard and Smith 2010). For that reason their experience of school has important implications for their development as socially and morally responsible citizens. In this chapter we take a look at what can often be thought of as the missing dimension in work on educational justice – the views of the students themselves. We will consider the legal and political framework which, at least in theory, entitles young people to a say in their educational destiny; before looking at the role that schools are playing through the teaching of Citizenship and other school-based activities. I then present the results from a large international research study which asked secondary school pupils about the extent to which they feel that their school experience is a fair one. In the final section we look at an alternative perspective on 'pupil voice' and consider the overly therapeutic nature of schooling.

The School I'd Like …

> The school I'd like would be where everyone's equal, and everybody's respected and their voices are heard.
>
> (Year 7 pupil, St Mary's school, Dorset, entry in the 2011 'The School I'd Like …' competition)

In 1967 *The Observer* newspaper held a competition inviting school children to imagine their ideal school. There were around 1,000 entries. More than thirty years later in 2001, *The Guardian* newspaper repeated the competition receiving over 15,000 entries, the best of which, along with their drawings, are compiled in the book *The School I'd like* (Burke and Grosvenor 2003). Pupils who participated in the competition had quite clear ideas about the sort of school they would like: quieter bells, desks with room for knees, maths classes in the swimming pool and fountains that spouted Fanta (Guardian, 2001a). They also wanted their opinions to be heard, something that as the above quotation shows students *still* wish for in 2011. The winning entries from the 2001 competition were combined in a Children's Manifesto which is reproduced in full in Box 6.1. This interest in asking school pupils about their views on their education, and indeed on their life more broadly, is a relatively recent development. It is also a powerful and popular one: it is enshrined in the UN Convention on the Rights of the Child, in the formation of a UK Youth Parliament and the appointment from 2001 onwards of Children's Commissioners for each of the four home countries (see below), it also prompted *The Guardian* to run a new round of the competition in 2011 (Guardian 2011a).

Box 6.1 The Children's Manifesto

The school we'd like is:

- A beautiful school with glass dome roofs to let in the light, uncluttered classrooms and brightly coloured walls.
- A comfortable school with sofas and beanbags, cushions on the floors, tables that don't scrape our knees, blinds that keep out the sun and quiet rooms where we can chill out.
- A safe school with swipe cards for the school gate, anti-bully alarms, first-aid classes and someone to talk to about our problems.
- A listening school with children on the governing body, class representatives and the chance to vote for the teachers.
- A flexible school without rigid timetables or exams, without compulsory homework, without a one-size-fits-all curriculum, so we can follow our own interests and spend more time on what we enjoy.
- A relevant school where we learn through experience, experiments and exploration, with trips to historic sites and teachers who have practical experience of what they teach.
- A respectful school where we are not treated as empty vessels to be filled with information, where teachers treat us as individuals, where children and adults can talk freely to each other and our opinion matters.
- A school without walls so we can go outside to learn, with animals to look after and wild gardens to explore.

- A school for everybody with boys and girls from all backgrounds and abilities, with no grading so we don't compete against each other but just do our best.

At the school we'd like, we'd have:

- Enough pencils and books for each child.
- Laptops so we could continue our work outside and at home.
- Drinking water in every classroom, and fountains of soft drinks in the playground.
- School uniforms of trainers, baseball caps and fleece tracksuits for boys and girls.
- Clean toilets that lock, with paper and soap, and flushes not chains.
- Fast-food school dinners and no dinner ladies.
- Large lockers to store our things.
- A swimming pool.

This is what we'd like. It is not an impossible dream.

Over the last two decades or so, the right of young people to be actively engaged in the matters which concern them has become an important issue for policy-makers and legislators. The Every Child Matters agenda in England has proposed a number of outcomes for all pupils, including being healthy and safe, making a positive contribution to society, and achieving economic well-being (Knowles 2009). Ofsted inspection criteria now require schools to demonstrate how they take into account the views of pupils. In Wales all schools must have a forum, usually a school council, where pupils can air their opinions and in 2008 the government made it mandatory that schools consult pupils on issues that concern them, from the way they are taught to behaviour and uniform policies (Stewart 2008). The rapid expansion of interest in pupil voice stems from the UN Convention on the Rights of the Child which was ratified by the UK in 1991. Its 42 Articles make it clear that children have the right to have a say about decisions which affect them and have their opinions listened to (UNICEF 2011). For example:

> *Article 12*: Children have the right to say what they think should happen, when adults are making decisions that affect them, and to have their opinions taken into account.
>
> *Article 15*: Children have the right to meet together and to join groups and organisations, as long as this does not stop other people from enjoying their rights.
>
> *Article 29*: Education should develop each child's personality and talents to the full. It should encourage children to respect their parents, and their own and other cultures.

The establishment of a Children's Commissioner for Wales in 2001 was the first step in providing young people in all four home nations with a representative who would champion their rights as set out in the UN Convention on the Rights of the Child (UNCRC). In Wales the role of the Children's Commissioner includes speaking out against inequality and discrimination, championing young people's rights and standing up in particular for those 'who are looked-after, ... have disabilities, gypsy traveller children and young people and those caught up in the youth justice system' (Children's Commissioner for Wales 2011). In addition to a network of school councils and pupil ambassadors the Children's Commissioner is active in involving children and young people in having a say in government policies. So, for example, to coincide with the Welsh Assembly government's consultation about proposals to charge for plastic bags, the Children's Commissioner's office ran a parallel consultation with young people asking for their views of the proposals. Another young people's organisation – Funky Dragon – works in partnership with the Welsh Assembly government to help children in Wales attain their rights under the UNCRC and to enable the voices of young people in Wales to be heard.

 Reflection

In an interview with the *Guardian* newspaper one of the authors of *The School I'd Like* had the following view:

> The school I'd like has now become the school I'd like my child to get into. Pupils have fallen out of the picture and parents are now in it. It's all about parental choice, not pupil choice. Pupil voice is being reduced and now seen as something problematic and in the way. (Birkett 2011)

Do you think this is true today?

Citizenship Education

Citizenship education was introduced as part of the National Curriculum for 11–16 year olds in England in September 2002. The inclusion of this subject as a compulsory element of the National Curriculum had important implications for developing students' perceptions about what it is to be part of an equitable and democratic society. The teaching of citizenship and democracy is, purportedly, needed to counter 'worrying levels of apathy, ignorance and cynicism about public life' (QCA 1998: 8). The final report from the advisory group on citizenship (the Crick Report) proposed a model for citizenship teaching that had, at its foundation, a curriculum based around the key concepts of 'fairness, rights and responsibilities' (QCA 1998: 20). One of the three inter-related components of citizenship teaching – social and moral responsibility (the other two being community involvement and political literacy) – seeks to encourage in pupils 'self-confidence and socially and morally responsible behaviour both in and beyond the classroom, towards those in authority and towards each other' (DfES 2002), to such an extent as to cause 'no less than a change in the political culture of this country both nationally and locally' (QCA 1998: 7).

In a House of Commons review of the Citizenship curriculum in 2007, the Education Select Committee described the teaching of Citizenship in schools as 'patchy at best' (House of Commons Education Select Committee 2007: 17) and expressed a recognition of the relatively lower status of Citizenship teaching in schools, a point reaffirmed by the trainee Citizenship teacher's commentary on the subject in Box 6.2. At the time of writing, the new Coalition government was reviewing the position of Citizenship education in school as part of their National Curriculum review. Whether the subject will survive the Review's stated aim of producing a slimmed down National Curriculum (DfE 2011f) remains to be seen.

Box 6.2 Why should we teach about Citizenship in school?

We should teach about Citizenship because it creates an opportunity for teaching about issues that are not traditionally covered in school, at least not in enough depth. Citizenship lessons cover so many topics including: community engagement, crime and conflict, democracy, identity and global citizenship. Citizenship lessons can be very flexible; because it covers everyday topics the curriculum can be changed depending on what is happening around the world or in a local area. This allows pupils to take more control of their lessons and they can often choose what they want to study depending on what is relevant to them. If there are particular issues associated with their community or school, Citizenship lessons can help pupils think about how to address them. For example, if there is a problem with gang culture locally, lessons could raise questions about why people join gangs, how it affects gang members and the people around them. Asking these questions will help make young people more aware of the reasons why people join gangs; it may even put them off joining gangs themselves.

Citizenship education should help create awareness of what it is to be a good citizen. It can cover almost any topic, because the most important thing about Citizenship lessons are not the topics themselves but the skills that young people learn. It teaches them to be critical about what they learn and encourages them to not always accept what they read or what they hear, but to develop their own opinions using all the information available to them. Citizenship education should also motivate children to become more active citizens, which means that they should take responsibilities for their own actions, but also to stand up for what they believe in and contribute to society in a positive way. If nothing else, Citizenship education is an important asset to helping children develop important skills which are necessary in other subjects but also in everyday life.

(Continued)

(Continued)

Unfortunately, my experience of teaching Citizenship so far has not been not very positive. At my first school placement I was allocated to teach eight Citizenship lessons. By the end of the placement I had only taught two lessons in total! Citizenship lessons seemed to have less value compared to other subjects. Every unexpected assembly or anything else that came up at the last minute was held during these lessons. Sometimes I came fully prepared to teach, only to find out that the lesson had been cancelled because of an assembly. Or I would arrive to be told that the pupils were already in an assembly and would be with me shortly, only for them to then arrive 20 minutes into the lesson. For me, it seemed that most things were more important than Citizenship. It is a shame that some schools have this attitude because this carries over to the children who then also see Citizenship education as a waste of time.

(Camilla Rehman, PGCE trainee in Citizenship Education)

Despite almost a decade of Citizenship education in school, concerns remain over young people's electoral participation and their engagement in civic activities such as volunteering; a situation which the current Prime Minister's 'Big Society' programme will also seek to address. Although it is interesting to see that in the government's first White Paper, *The Importance of Teaching* (DfE 2010b), there is no mention of Citizenship education in schools. In addition, the regular national Citizenship Survey was discontinued in January 2011.

In the 2010 General Election only around 49 per cent of young people aged 18–25 voted and despite campaigns to increase the numbers registered to vote, this group remains the least likely to participate (Keating et al. 2010; Guardian 2010a). Since 2002 the Citizenship Education Longitudinal Study (CELS) has been tracking how citizenship and citizenship education has been practised in schools and by young people. The final report from CELS was published in 2010 and concluded that citizenship education could have a positive impact on young people's lives (Keating et al. 2010). The research found a 'marked and steady increase in civic and political participation' (p. 60) with students engaging in activities such as signing petitions, electing pupil/school council members and fund-raising for charities and good causes. On the other hand, the research reported a 'hardening' (p. 61) of attitudes towards equality and society, particularly towards issues such as immigration and benefit payments, yet at the same time they report enhanced support towards issues such as human rights. This led the authors of the report to conclude that:

> ... there is still some work to be done on influencing young people's citizenship attitudes and their levels of engagement, efficacy and trust in the political arena. (Keating et al. 2010: 62)

Encouraging children and young people to become active citizens and concerned about the matters which affect them is of course a very important dimension in attempts to make their lives fairer and more equitable. Another way is to engage them in a dialogue about their views and experiences of school and then to use their ideas to help improve schools. We consider this aspect of pupil voice in the next section.

Pupils' Experience of Fairness in School: A Research Study

Large-scale international studies such as the IEA Civic Education Study have tried to gain a clearer understanding of students' concepts of democracy and citizenship and how this varies across different nations (Civic Education Study 2001). The 1999 phase of the Civic Education Study surveyed around 120,000 pupils aged 14 and 17–18. One key finding to emerge from this study was that schools that embraced democratic values by promoting an open climate for discussion, for example through school councils, were more likely to be effective in promoting both civic knowledge and civic engagement (Torney-Purta et al. 2001). While there are many lessons to be learnt from studies of this type, their focus tends to be on issues of civic responsibility and civic engagement particularly outside the school. There is comparatively less research into how pupils experience fairness and unfairness in their own schools and societies. In this section I will present the findings from an international study which examined this very hope.

To understand more about equity in education, it is important to ask the participants themselves. The views of pupils are still surprisingly scarce in education research, despite pupils' clear competence as commentators (Wood 2003). This absence is perhaps particularly marked for pupils in already marginalised groups (Rose and Shevlin 2004; Reay 2006; Lewis et al. 2006). Our interest in the present study was to examine how systems of fairness operate within schools and how this affects pupils' experiences and perspectives about education in general. Pupils' feelings of injustice are important. They are important for moral reasons, because it is implicit in the basic conception of the modern educational system that every child matters and their needs are of equal importance. Pupils' feelings are important for academic reasons, because unfairly treated pupils are likely to react in a way that will negatively affect their learning and, more generally, pupils in classes and schools where a lot of injustice exists are less likely to learn well. Their feelings are important for educational reasons, because unfairness may harm the personal development of pupils (lowering self-esteem, for instance). They are also important for civic reasons, because unfairly treated pupils may develop inadequate conceptions of justice and other attitudes or beliefs detrimental to social cohesion and participation in active democracy (Gorard and Smith 2010).

Around 14,000 14-year-old pupils in around 450 schools took part in this research. Those who were involved came from six different countries: England, France, Belgium, Italy, the Czech Republic and Japan. Full details of the study can be found in Gorard and Smith (2010). Pupils were asked to complete a short questionnaire which asked them about their experiences of fair treatment in school and then gave them the opportunity to provide examples of situations where they had been treated fairly as well as unfairly. The following sections will summarise the key thoughts of the nearly 3,000 English pupils who took part in this research.

Treating Pupils Consistently and Fairly

The majority of pupils who participated in the study told us that they had a positive relationship with their teachers, and that their teachers tended to treat them fairly. Most reported that their efforts in school were rewarded fairly and that their opinions were treated with respect. However, while the majority of pupils report that their experiences of school are largely fair, there were nevertheless large numbers who disagreed. For example, not all pupils felt that they were treated fairly or with respect, or that their teachers were interested in their well-being. One of the clearest areas of concern was their perception that teachers treated certain groups of pupils differently and were inconsistent in their allocation of rewards and punishments. Indeed, the notion that both punishments and rewards could be allocated unevenly despite similar circumstances was one which generated the most complaints from pupils. This can be seen in the comments below:

> I expressed an opinion in class, my teacher disregarded it, then another pupil said the same thing and she congratulated them. My opinion was not respected. (Female pupil)

> At this one incident I got a detention for looking at the clock by Ms T. I think that is unfair because it was a harsh punishment and in most people's opinion I did nothing wrong. (Male pupil)

> My chemistry teacher sent me out of the classroom for the whole lesson for sitting in the wrong seat. (Sex unknown)

> My teacher sent me out of the classroom (not school policy) for sneezing in class. The same teacher earlier on in the year sent me out again for no apparent reason. Both times he claimed I was attention seeking. (Male pupil)

> [Pupil] threw a chair at my head I had eight stitches. He got two days internal suspension. I have sworn at a teacher in the past and got a week external suspension. (Sex unknown)

> When a pupil can wear their own coat throughout the class and another pupil wears a ring and is asked to remove it. Certain pupils are allowed to sleep in lessons. (Female pupil)

> In our school we recently had a new PE teacher. I forgot my PE kit and so did another girl in our class. She fined me £2.50 and not the other girl saying that it was her first time for forgetting the PE kit. (Female pupil)

It is episodes like these that help pupils decide whether or not a school or a teacher is unfair. The biggest complaints from the pupils came when they felt that they were not punished equally for the same offence and also when the punishment appeared disproportionate to what might have taken place. So, for example, being given detention for looking at the clock was deemed unfair. It was not that the pupils objected to being punished, rather that they wanted such punishment, and any reward of course, to be distributed proportionately and clearly.

The pupils who took part in this study were also particularly concerned about the unequal attention that teachers gave to different groups of pupils. Their comments spanned a range of different pupil characteristics from the badly behaved, to the lower attainers, to the more academically successful – with the consensus being that teachers ought to treat all pupils in the same way in most respects. These comments give some indication of the extent to which pupils regard the unequal treatment of pupils to be an area of concern:

> I don't like the way that the least intelligent pupils get loads of praise and awards for doing nothing just because they're unintelligent. (Female pupil)

> How the naughty children get more attention and get highly praised when they manage to produce the same amount of work as the rest of the class which they should be doing anyway. (Female pupil)

> I had finished some work and asked my teacher to read it and see if I could improve, but she said 'no' because she was dealing with other pupils who were misbehaving. (Male pupil)

> Schools are not fair at all. If there are idiots in your class and you can't do your work, the teachers are always paying more attention to them. And two weeks ago in P school, all the badly behaved pupils went bowling and had a McDonald's and all the behaved pupils had nothing. Do you call that fair? (Male pupil)

As well as taking issue with inconsistent treatment of different groups of pupils, the presence of teachers' 'favourites' particularly vexed the English pupils. In fact, the vast majority of these pupils told us that their teachers had pupils whom they favoured, in particular those perceived to be hard-working. This was borne out by their comments.

> I try really hard in all my tests and homework, but I don't get grades which reflect the effort I put into it. Also some teachers have their favourites and ignore others. (Female pupil)

> When teachers go to their favourite pupils and then never get time to see you then ask for you to stay after school to get help, when you have after-school activities – happened to me it's unfair. (Female pupil)

Undertaking this research showed us that asking pupils about their experiences of school in this context does not lead to excessive complaining but rather to what appears to be a considered account of those actions, by their teachers, which pupils see as being unfair and inequitable. The young people who participated in this study generally regarded their school experience as being fair. Many told us that they enjoy their education, having been treated well at school, and feel that their learning has purpose. Most have good friends, and only a minority report unpleasant episodes such as bullying. Many pupils trust their teachers and find them helpful and supportive. On the other hand, a significant minority report that their school experience is not fair and, in particular, observe that their teachers were inconsistent and unfair when administering punishments and rewards. Indeed this inconsistent treatment of different groups of pupils by their teachers was the biggest 'complaint' that the participants raised.

Do 'Disadvantaged' Pupils Experience Fairness Differently?

Of additional interest in this study were the experiences of those young people who might be considered to be the most disadvantaged in school, such as those from less wealthy homes, recent immigrants and the academically less successful. You will know from your other studies as well as from the earlier chapters in this book that certain groups of pupils are not as academically successful in school as others and that these inequalities tend to persist throughout schooling and into adulthood (see Chapters 7 and 8).

That the school experiences of certain groups of pupils might not be as fair as that of their peers is summed up by one of the respondents when asked to report any instances when they had been treated unfairly:

> Personally no! As I am Caucasian, middle-class and well-spoken, if I was not however, this section might be rather different.

However, looking at the responses of those pupils who belong to potentially more vulnerable groups suggests that their experiences of fair treatment are *not* appreciably more negative than their peers. For example, the responses of those who had different cultural experiences at home – in terms of the language they spoke or whether they were born in the UK – were similar to the other pupils (Table 6.1).

This is an important finding because it tells us that, in many respects, pupil background, their family and the type of school they attend (or even for those who do not attend school) are all unrelated to their experiences of justice and injustice in school. This, of course, is in contrast to school academic outcomes, which as we have seen in Chapter 4, are heavily stratified according to pupil background characteristics.

Table 6.1 Percentage of students who agreed with the statements

	Time lived in Britain		Language spoken at home	
	Always	After born	English	Other
I was always treated fairly by my teachers	40	40	40	39
I trusted my teachers to be fair	59	55	59	62
Generally speaking, school was a fair place	47	45	46	52
School has been a waste of time for me	7	8	7	7

Source: Gorard and Smith (2010).

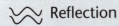 Reflection

Findings such as these might help us develop additional ways of deciding whether or not schools are 'effective' that go beyond simply looking at examination results. So if a school is able to demonstrate that it is able to raise pupils' aspirations and their enjoyment of school, encourage active citizenship and respect for others and in turn be happy welcoming places for all pupils regardless of who they are and where they come from, then might this be the sort of education system that we should be aspiring to in this country? What are your views on this? Do you think that measuring happiness or civic engagement is too subjective? Or perhaps you think that these are characteristics that need to be developed outside the school, in the home or community, and have no place in schools whose primary function should be the development of academic knowledge and skills?

Activity

In this research project, to help how pupils constructed different notions of fairness, we gave them a number of small scenarios and asked them which response they thought was the fairest. One of these scenarios is given here:

Bella has special educational needs and can often be very disruptive in class. In Bella's school, if pupils behave in lessons they are given reward points which means they can go on a trip at the end of term. In maths Bella was badly behaved at the start of the lesson and Mr J the teacher threatened to send her to the head teacher. This made Bella settle down and she worked quietly for the rest of the lesson and finished all her work. At the end of the lesson, she was given a reward point.

(a) This was fair because Bella has difficulties which make it hard for her to concentrate in class. It is right that she is treated differently and rewarded for her improved behaviour.

(b) Bella should have behaved for the whole lesson just like the rest of the class. It is not fair to reward pupils who behave badly.

Which response would you favour? One that uses a principle of discrimination (that equal treatment is not fair and resources should be allocated according to need) or an egalitarian response (that equal treatment is fair)? You might be interested to know that in the research project this scenario divided opinion the most.

Giving Pupils too Much Voice?

In this section we reconsider some of the issues that are raised by current preoccupations with 'pupil voice' and offer an alternative perspective which asks whether perhaps this idea of valuing the voice of pupils has gone a bit too far.

This is a question that might be prompted from reading these comments from pupils who contributed to the 'The School I'd Like ...' competition:

> They do ask what we'd like sometimes. When we were getting a new teacher, we had a lesson from three teachers and we were asked which one we liked the best. They did choose her ... (Year 6 pupil, featured in the *Education Guardian*, 25 January 2011: 2)

> In my perfect school there would still be rules, but they would guide us, not confine us. There would be no grading, praise only for working hard and not your mental capability ... We would discuss our opinions in every lesson. Teachers and pupils would be equal ... (Lower secondary competition winner, *The Guardian* 2001)

So should teachers and pupils be equal and should pupils sit on interview panels and have a say in choosing their teacher? The answers to these questions reveal much about our current preoccupation with childhood. Part of this might be seen as an over-indulgence of youth that encourages young people to have too much say. Consider, for example, the popularity of websites such as Rate My Teacher where pupils are encouraged to mark their teacher/subject according to how helpful and popular they might be. On the one hand, this might be an effective way to provide pupils with an anonymous forum to praise or to criticise their teachers. An alternative view is that such websites are tantamount to cyber bullying and enable pupils to spread rumours and slurs against their teachers (see, for example, BBC 2006; *The Guardian* 2007): See Box 6.3 for an example of a school based intervention that encourages students to access their teacher's teaching.

Box 6.3 INSTED at Beauchamp School, Leicestershire

Since 2006 Beauchamp School has been running the INSTED programme in which the pupils observe teachers teaching and evaluate the strengths of their lessons. Nominated pupils are provided with two one-and-a-half hour training sessions before being able to observe lessons. Pupil observers are drawn from across the ability and behaviour range:

> We try very hard to make sure that lesson observers represent the full ability and not just those at the top end. Sometimes having students as lesson observers who have something of a reputation as being disruptive in class can be a very useful learning experience!' (Beauchamp College 2010: 13)

Modelled on Ofsted's approach, students record their observations and although the name of the teacher is not included in the report, students are required to feed back the strengths of the lesson to the teacher, as well as offer targets for further development. The ethos of INSTED is to provide an alternative view of lessons with pupils often noticing different aspects of teaching which are not often picked up by teacher peer observers. The school has produced a guide for other schools interested in adopting this process saying that: 'We think it is time that the pupil voice became just as important as the teacher voice' (Beauchamp College 2010: 27).

What are your thoughts about strategies which seek to promote pupil voice and well-being in this way? Do you agree with the critics that they undermine the professional's autonomy and infantilise children and young people?

The spectacle of over-indulgent parenting has also received much attention recently. Take the helicopter parents who hover constantly around their children afraid in case they come to harm, as recounted by a head teacher in the *Sunday Times* newspaper:

> A girl in Year 9 is seen smoking by two members of staff and it is an open-and-shut case that she has broken school rules. However, it ceases to be an open-and-shut case when the helicopter parent phones you to say that his 'little girl' was only 'holding the cigarette' for a friend who was standing beside her at the time.
>
> You are sceptical about the claim, but you go back to the members of staff who saw the girl to check again. They are adamant that the girl was actually smoking the cigarette. You return to the helicopter parent with the update and – surprise, surprise – they tell you that the two members of staff are 'mistaken' because (and you frequently hear this) 'my daughter has never told me a lie in her life'. (Macnaughton 2008)

It is a phenomenon which has extended even to early adulthood, where helicopter parents deal with their son's or daughter's university application, phone their university department to complain when an exam has been rescheduled, or negotiate pay settlements for their offspring's first job (MacLeod 2008; BBC 2008).

Helicopter parenting styles sit in contrast to the tough parenting approach favoured by Amy Chua in her 2011 book *The Battle Hymn of the Tiger Mother*. This autobiographical account of how Chua raised her two daughters caused much incredulity when it was published in the USA, where her 'Chinese parenting' approach also revealed much about US insecurities about the economic dominance of China coupled with concerns about the quality of the American school system (Murphy Paul 2011). An indication of the tough parenting approach adopted by Chua can be seen from the extract below which is taken from an interview with the author that was published by *Time* magazine (Luscombe 2011).

> *Interviewer:* What has provoked the most reaction?
>
> *Chua:* The story I'm getting most flak for her is one I stand by. My daughters find the trouble I'm getting in for it incredibly funny. My kids were maybe seven and four and my husband had forgotten my birthday so at the last

minute we went to this mediocre Italian restaurant and he said 'OK, girls you both have a little surprise for mommy.' And my daughter Lulu pulls out a card, but the card was just a piece of paper folded crookedly in half with a big smiley face and it said Happy Birthday Mom. And I looked at it and I gave it back and I said 'This isn't good enough. I want something that you put a little bit more time into.' So I rejected her birthday card. People can't believe I rejected this handmade card. But she knew as well as I did that it took her about two seconds to do it. That's the story that's coming off as the most outrageous, which in our family is like a standing joke.

There is an important point here. The virtue and value of listening to children as outlined in documents such as the UN Convention of the Rights of the Child are not in dispute. There are children and young people in Britain, as elsewhere, whose lives are made more difficult and challenging by their peers and even by the adults who are supposed to care for them. This is not the issue. Rather it is the over-indulgence of parents and the infantilisation of childhood that are of concern (Furedi 2009). Not only do these have the potential to undermine both the authority and professionalism of teachers, one might argue that they may also undermine the voice of vulnerable children and young people.

Therapeutic Education and Social Justice

As we discussed at the start of this chapter, interest in the value of 'pupil voice' has been growing for the past two decades. More recently, however, this focus has begun to take a 'therapeutic' turn, particularly with regard to the development of pupils' emotional well-being. This is an area which perhaps unsurprisingly has attracted a great deal of attention from policy-makers whose notion of social justice connects 'emotional well-being to a view that social exclusion emerges from destructive influences that damage self-esteem and emotional well-being and is therefore a key characteristic of social injustice' (Ecclestone and Hayes 2008: 373). Such interests are often based on a 'story' which goes something like this:

> Children are more miserable today than they have been for years. Because they are miserable, they are disruptive at school, cannot motivate themselves to learn, and are prey to destructive (including self-destructive) behaviour. Their futures look bleak unless we take steps to improve their emotional well-being now. We need to teach them how to overcome negative feelings, how to keep calm, how to value themselves and others. (Cigman 2010: 11)

The result for schools has been expensive courses in learning to learn happiness, well-being and emotional literacy. And activities such as Social and Emotional Aspects of Learning (SEAL), Philosophy for Children and circle time have mushroomed. This 'rise' of therapeutic education has, according to Eccleston and Hayes (2008), left children learning that 'life, with all its trivial and serious tribulations, mundane and difficult low moments, "sucks" and requires an array of "therapeutic support workers" in the form of peer buddies, theatre educators ... life coaches, or specialist counsellors' (p. 155). Rather than encouraging young people to be aware of each other's feelings; 'therapeutic education elevates everyday feelings of uncertainty, vulnerability, discomfort or lack of confidence and depicts them as "treatable" (p. 155).

Summary

This chapter has considered another aspect of social justice in school: the experiences of the pupils themselves. Over the last twenty years or so, the importance of what has been termed 'pupil voice' has grown. The right of children and young people to have a say in the matters that affect them is enshrined in the United Nations Convention on the Rights of the Child and is embodied by the Children's Commissioners whose role is to champion young people's rights. The teaching of citizenship is yet another example of the importance of schooling in helping prepare the next generation of 'socially and morally responsible citizens'. Our recent research into pupils' experiences of school suggests that they seem to have a clear notion about what constitutes a fair and equitable national education system. Most pupils enjoy their education, having been treated well at school, and feel that their learning has purpose. However it was also clear that for many pupils, their school experience was not a fair one but was one where teachers were inconsistent and unfair when administering punishments and rewards. There is, however, a growing backlash to the over-use of pupil voice, particularly in initiatives which critics see as being over-therapeutic.

 Reflection

The outcomes of research into pupil experiences of fairness and justice raise many fundamental questions about how schools operate as mini societies (Gorard 2011).

For example, should schools and teachers discriminate between pupils? We would probably not want schools to use more funds to educate boys than girls. But we might want schools to use more funds for pupils with learning difficulties. Should a teacher be allowed to punish a pupil who misbehaves, or reward a pupil who has shown talent or effort? If so, then the teacher is being discriminating.

If we stick too closely to a principle of equality of opportunity then the likely result is that there will be large inequalities in outcomes. Students who need additional help would not receive it and would perhaps not be able to perform at a similar level to their peers who might not need additional help. So is it fair that teachers treat pupils differently and in doing so risk some of the criticism implied in the comments above?

(Continued)

(Continued)

Contrast Gorard's view that schools act as mini societies with that of Mary Warnock in the previous chapter who argued that schools are not 'microcosms' of society. Which, in your view, is the more accurate representation of what schools ought to be like?

Further reading

Ecclestone, K. and Hayes, D. (2008) *The Dangerous Rise of Therapeutic Education*. London: Routledge.

Gorard, S. and Smith, E. (2010) *Equity in Education: An International Perspective*. Palgrave Macmillan.

Burke, C. and Grosvenor, I. (2003) *The School I'd Like*. London: Routledge.

Osler, A. (2010) *Students' Perspectives on Schooling*. Maidenhead: Open University Press.

Higher education and social justice

Education is the most powerful tool we have in achieving social justice.

(John Denham, former Universities Secretary, Universities UK Annual Conference, September 2008)

In 1963 just 8.5 per cent of the British population went to university; by 2010 this figure was nearer to 40 per cent (Chowdry et al. 2010; Attwood 2010). Over the last fifty years higher education in the UK has moved from being an elite to a mass experience. The sector now contributes around £59 billion to the economy and attracts over 340,000 foreign students (Department for Innovation, Universities and Skills 2009). The benefits of a university education are not just academic: we are told that studying in higher education will significantly influence one's life chances and earning potential (Department for Innovation, Universities and Skills 2009), that graduates are more likely to have better jobs, enjoy better health and live longer than those who do not have a degree (Marmot Review 2010). Indeed, through policies and initiatives to both increase and widen participation (for example, DfES 2003b), successive governments have reinforced the notion that going to university is a 'great way to get on' (Denham 2008). In this chapter we will consider the impact that the 'massification' of higher education has had on the participation of groups of students who have traditionally been less likely to go to university. We consider who has benefited from the remarkable expansion of the sector and who has been left behind. We will begin our discussion with some of the key government policies which have sought, over the last fifty years, to increase participation and subsequently also to widen it. We then look at the impact of such policies on the characteristics of those who take part.

The Move to Mass Higher Education

In 1999, Tony Blair pledged to 'care about educating the many':

> In today's world, there is no such thing as too clever. The more you know, the
> further you'll go. The forces of conservatism, the elite, have held us back for too
> long ... so today I set a target of 50 per cent of young adults going into higher
> education in the next century. (Tony Blair, Speech to the Annual Labour Party
> Conference, Bournemouth, 28 September 1999).

Over a decade later, and in the year that his 50 per cent target is supposed to be
met, the higher education sector is faced with funding cuts of unprecedented
magnitude. This, according to some commentators, will mean that Blair's ambi-
tions for HE and its contribution to 'a model 21st century nation, based not on
privilege, class or background, but on the equal worth of all' will be unlikely to
be achieved (Attwood 2010). Whatever its future prospects may be, it is clear
that the rapid expansion of the sector over the last quarter of a century has
changed the face of higher education in the UK. Indeed, since 1986, the number
of UK-based candidates who apply to study at university has doubled to almost
500,000. There has been a proliferation of courses, degree providers and opportunities for further study – from foundation degrees to 'courses in media studies
and surf science' (BBC 2003; *The Guardian* 2003). Alongside this expansion has
come the inevitable question of who will shoulder the costs of higher education.
Is it fair, for example, that a taxpayer who did not go to university should be
expected to pay the fees of someone fortunate enough to attend? Or in other
words 'Should the dustman continue to subsidise the doctor or should the doctor contribute towards the cost of their own education?' (BBC 2002). In the
aftermath of the Browne Review into Higher Education funding (BIS 2010d) and
subsequent cuts to the sector, these are important questions.

To put the current debate around HE funding and participation into context it is worth looking briefly at the recent historical context behind the mass
expansion of higher education in the UK.

After the Second World War, the number of young people studying at university increased rapidly: from around 40,000 students in the 1920s to well over
80,000 by the 1950s (Committee on Higher Education 1963; table 3, para. 46).
This increase resulted in the founding of seven new universities at York, Lancaster,
Warwick, Sussex, East Anglia, Essex and Kent in the early 1960s. The expansion
in the student population was partly a result of the economic and social changes
that followed the Second World War but was also a consequence of the 1944
Education Act, which increased the number of selective grammar school places
and subsequently opened up the route into higher education for an expanding
middle class (Archer et al. 2003; Gillard 2007). In 1963 the government commissioned Lord Robbins to review the medium- and long-term expansion of higher
education. The Robbins Committee paid particular consideration to how the
sector would cope with the predicted shortfall of university places caused by the
large numbers of young people who were born after the War and who would be
eligible to enter higher education between 1965 and 1968 (Committee on Higher

Education 1963). The report projected that by 1980–81 the number of full-time students would rise to about 560,000 (Committee on Higher Education 1963; table 30) and recommended the immediate expansion of the university sector.

The university landscape of the 1960s was very different to that of today. Then there were just 21 universities (Watson 2006) compared with 165 institutions of higher education in 2009 (HESA 2010). It was, however, a highly socially segregated system that catered overwhelmingly for the children of the wealthy and/or the highly educated. For example, 45 per cent of all entrants to full-time higher education in 1961/2 came from a higher professional/ managerial background, while for those whose father had a skilled-manual occupation the figure was just 4 per cent (Committee on Higher Education 1963; para. 139). In addition, the proportion of university students whose fathers had stayed in education until they were 18 was eight times higher than for those students whose father had left school before they were 16 (Committee on Higher Education 1963; table 22, para. 140). Thus the university system at the time of the Robbins Report was arguably a system for the elite, starkly segregated according to social background. While Robbins recognised that 'the reserves of untapped ability may be greatest in the poorest sections of the community' (Committee on Higher Education 1963; para. 142) there were no specific recommendations about how participation from the most 'disadvantaged' sections of the community should be increased.

It wasn't until the 1990s that the sentiment for change became more apparent with the publication of the Dearing Report in 1997. This report from the National Committee of Inquiry into Higher Education (NCIHE 1997) placed an emphasis on widening access to the expanding university system. Its aims were explicit: that the future of higher education in the UK would require institutions to

> ... encourage and enable all students – whether they demonstrate the highest intellectual potential or whether they have struggled to reach the threshold of higher education – to achieve beyond their expectations. (para. 5)

The report promoted an agenda of *widening participation* whereby groups which had routinely been excluded from higher education – those from lower socioeconomic groups, had disabilities or who came from certain ethnic minority groups – would be encouraged to participate. It echoed the political sentiment of the time: from Tony Blair's 'education, education, education' to this from Gordon Brown:

> I believe that Britain has often in the past also been held back by an ... often heard assertion that 'more means worse', that to educate more and more young people is wasteful because they simply don't have the talent to benefit. And instead of talking of a pool of untapped talent, some people have talked of a pool of tapped untalent. (Brown 2007)

In order to explore the moves towards mass higher education that were prompted by reports such as Dearing's, it is helpful to look at changes in the numbers and types of people who apply and are accepted to study at university. High-quality data on this topic are available as far back as the 1980s.

Who Participates in Higher Education?

The modern story of higher education in the UK can be seen by tracking participation since the late 1980s. This was a time of great change for the education systems in England and Wales, not least because the 1988 Education Act led to the replacement of the old O-level/CSE qualification system with the GCSE. One of the key effects of the 1988 Education Act was that subjects such as Mathematics, English and Science became compulsory up to the age of 16. A second consequence was an expansion in the number of vocational courses for those aged 14–19 (Docking 1996). Both of these developments increased the number of young people who were 'eligible' to study in Higher education.

From 1986, applications to universities and the former polytechnics[1] were made through the Universities Central Council on Admissions (UCCA) and the Polytechnics Central Admissions Service (PCAS). Since the merger of these two organisations in 1993, all candidates wishing to apply to the UK higher education sector have had to make their application through the Universities Central Admissions Service (UCAS). As we can see from Figure 7.1, the number of people who apply and are accepted to study at university has increased steadily over the last twenty years. This growth in acceptances is mirrored by growth in the number of applicants as the number of university places available increases to accommodate demand. However, it is still the case that more candidates apply to study at university than are eventually accepted. Despite media reports complaining that 209,000 'degree hopefuls' missed out on their university place in 2010 (for example, BBC 2010f) 75 per cent of all applicants accepted their places at university in that year compared with only 48 per cent of applicants in 1987 (UCAS 2010; Smith 2010b).

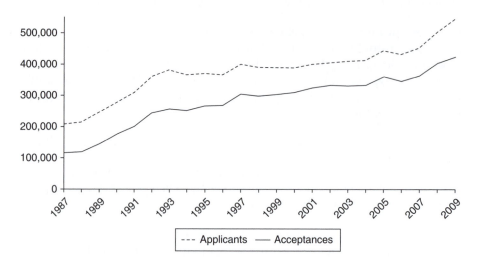

Figure 7.1 Applicants and acceptances, all home candidates 1987–2009

Source: Smith (2010b).

This expansion of the higher education system is reflected in a quadrupling of the number of candidates offered places to study at undergraduate level. This increase is particularly apparent among some previously under-represented groups. In 1986, 47,696 women accepted places on undergraduate courses; by 2009 this had risen to well over 200,000. The early 1990s saw the end of a long-established trend of HE institutions recruiting more male candidates. Now more female candidates are accepted to university than men (Figure 7.2).

The expansion of HE has not just meant that more UK domiciled students remain in education for longer. The UK is the second most popular destination (after the USA) for students from overseas who wish to study abroad. According to the Higher Education Statistics Agency (HESA), in 2008/9 there were 251,310 students who were born outside the European Union studying in the UK (an increase of 10 per cent over the previous year); the majority of these students come from India and Nigeria (HESA 2010). International students studying in the UK contribute around £5.5 billion to the country's national income (Department for Innovation, Universities and Skills 2009).

Yet as we shall see below, despite more students going to university than ever before, inequalities in participation have endured over the past fifty years, with significant groups being routinely under-represented (Stevenson and Lang 2010). Participation has long been differentiated in terms of socioeconomic status (Bynner 1992; Fisher 2010) as well as other 'pre-adult' social, geographic and historical factors such as year of birth and type of school attended (see, Gorard et al. 2007). Contemporary widening participation initiatives, such as those introduced below, seek to break such cycles and ensure that, in the context of raising levels of attainment, access to higher education is attainable and equitable for all.

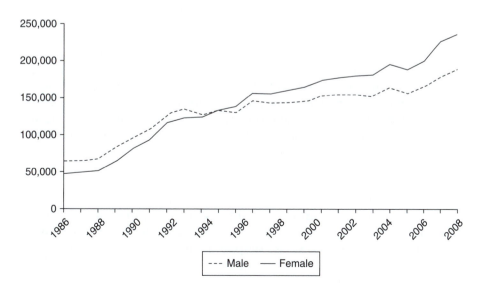

Figure 7.2 Male and female acceptances to all full-time undergraduate courses, 1986–2009
Source: Smith (2012).

Widening Participation in UK Higher Education

In 1997 the report of the National Committee of Inquiry into Higher Education, chaired by Lord Dearing, was explicit about the need to open up access to higher education for those who were least likely to attend:

> ... it should be an objective of policy to see that those groups who are currently under-represented in higher education come to be properly represented: *as participation increases so it must widen*. (NCIHE 1997; para. 7.21, emphasis added)

Since the publication of Lord Dearing's report in 1997 there have been a number of initiatives that have aimed, either directly or indirectly, to increase participation in higher education in general and, in particular, among those social groups who traditionally have been less likely to participate (e.g. NAO 2002; DfES 2003b, 2006; Department of Trade and Industry 1998). This has led to a range of initiatives including Aimhigher (see Box 7.1), Foundation Degrees, Train to Gain and Lifelong Learning Networks.

Box 7.1 Aimhigher

The Aimhigher programme is a series of initiatives designed to raise awareness of higher education, particularly among groups who are underrepresented in university. Activities take place across England and include visits to university campuses, residential schemes and summer schools. In 2009–10 1,210,362 potential HE students were involved in Aimhigher activities (Hansard 2011). But evaluations of Aimhigher point to mixed success. The very diversity and small-scale nature of many Aimhigher programmes make comparisons difficult (Passy and Morris 2010) and while evaluations show that participants enjoy the Aimhigher programmes and report an increased interest in progressing to HE, the research does not tend to follow participants as they make their decisions post-18. This makes it difficult to know whether or not these students eventually progressed to university and any role that Aimhigher might have played in informing their decisions (McCaig et al. 2006; Passy and Morris 2010). Recent research by Chilosi et al. (2010) which included an element of student tracking does, however, suggest that Aimhigher has a positive impact on HE applications. However, Aimhigher is another programme to fall victim to current spending cuts and ceased to be funded by the government from July 2011. Instead, widening participation programmes like Aimhigher will be funded by each university (Hansard 2010a).

In addition to programmes and initiatives, there has also been direct financial support offered to disadvantaged students, for example in the form of Opportunity Bursaries, aimed at removing the economic barriers to higher education (NAO 2008). However, despite an increase in the proportion of young people entering the sector, inequalities in participation persist (see, for example, the report of the Panel on Fair Access to the Professions chaired by MP Alan Millburn (Cabinet Office 2009)). According to Furlong and Cartmel (2009) simply looking at the numbers of students who participate obscures part of the story; instead, higher education is stratified in many other ways: in terms of the type of institution students study at, the courses they follow and even the extent to which they engage with their degree.

Even though higher education has been transformed from an 'elite to a mass experience' (Fulong and Cartmel 2009: 121), the experience of students from less well-off families is 'impoverished' in comparison to those from the more affluent middle classes. Indeed, going to university has become part of the 'normal taken for granted experience of the middle classes' (Furlong and Cartmel 2009: 121, see also Blanden and Machin 2004). And it is still the case that fewer than one in five young people from the most disadvantaged areas enter higher education compared to more than one in two for the most advantaged areas (HEFCE 2010). Research in Scotland by Raffe et al. (2006) comes to a similar conclusion about social-class inequalities in participation. Their research looked at levels of attainment at age 16 through to participation in higher education and shows similar and consistent patterns: that young people from what they call 'working-class' homes achieved at lower levels than their peers from managerial/professional backgrounds and, perhaps unsurprisingly, were also less likely to stay in education. Work by Mangan et al. (2010) also found that social-class background was strongly associated with the type of university to which students apply and this was particularly linked to the type of school that students attended. Indeed, as we will see below, students who attend a school in the independent sector were far more likely to study at an elite university when compared with students educated in the state sector.

In short, recent research suggests that two things have happened to university participation in the UK. First that the numbers of people entering HE from under-represented groups have increased and applicants who have the required grades have usually been able to secure a place. This of course is good news. However, on the other hand, there is compelling evidence to suggest that many students from these previously under-represented groups are less likely to study the most prestigious subjects at elite universities. This notion of *horizontal stratification* of higher education is important and we can see these patterns of inequality for ourselves if we look at data on the types of students who apply to different courses. In the examples below we look a little more closely at the types of subjects and institutions at which different groups of students study.

Example 1: Do Non-traditional Age Students Study at 'less' Prestigious Universities?

The percentage of full-time students aged over the age of 21 who are accepted to study in different types of universities is shown in Table 7.1. The 'old' universities are those which held university status before the 1992 Further and Higher Education Act and include the elite Russell Group institutions (such as Oxford, Manchester, Birmingham and Bristol) as well as the universities which belong to the 1994 group of smaller research-intensive institutions (including York, Leicester and Exeter)[2]. Although judging the quality of different institutions is extremely problematic, the 'old' (or pre-1992)

Table 7.1 Percentage of non-traditional age full-time undergraduates

	All students	
	1996	2009
All students	19	16
'Old' universities	13	10
Former polytechnics	25	21

Source: UCAS (1996, 2009).

universities traditionally have offered the most 'academic' courses and asked for the highest entry grades, in comparison with the (former) polytechnics that traditionally offered more vocational courses. Of course, being an elite research university does not guarantee high standards of teaching and student care. What Table 7.1 does tell us though is that students who are of non-traditional university age (i.e. aged 22 and over) are more likely to attend the less prestigious universities: 21 per cent of them did this in 2009, compared with 10 per cent who attended the more 'elite' institutions. It is also interesting to see that the percentage of older students who have entered higher education since 1996 has also declined slightly (from 19 per cent of all entrants in 1996 to 16 per cent in 2009). In many ways this fall in the number of older students studying at university over time is not surprising. One explanation for this is that early initiatives to widen access will already have attracted older students who were set on a university education. As these have passed through the system, the number of potential non-traditional age students who might attend but have not yet done so will decrease and we will see participation rates fall – what Gorard et al. (2002) call the 'conveyor belt effect'.

Example 2: What Subjects do Students From Different Educational Backgrounds Study?

We can see similar inequalities when we look at the types of courses that are studied by students from different educational backgrounds. Table 7.2 shows the different types of subjects that are studied by students who had been educated in the independent school sector. Around 10 per cent of all full-time undergraduate students in 2008/9 had attended an independent school, compared with around 7 per cent of the whole school-age population. But their choice of subject is quite different from students who went to state school. They are more likely to study prestigious courses such as Medicine, Economics and Languages and less likely to study more vocational courses such as Nursing or Education. For instance, almost one third of all medical students attended independent schools. You can also see that Law students from independent schools are more likely to attend the elite Russell Group universities: 17 per cent of Law students in Russell Group universities attended independent schools, compared with 7 per cent of all Law students.

Table 7.2 Percentage of undergraduates who attended independent schools, selected subject areas 2008/9

	Students educated in the independent sector (%)
All subjects	10
Medicine	29
Economics	23
European Language and Literature	25
Nursing	2
Education	3
Law (all institutions)	7
Law (Russell Group)	17

Source: HESA 2010.

Example 3: Do students from different occupational backgrounds study different subjects?

The final example takes a look at the subjects that students from higher managerial and professional occupational backgrounds study in comparison with other students. Around 16 per cent of students come from this occupational background but they are more likely to study elite subjects such as Medicine, Physics and Mathematics and less likely to study subjects like Computer Science and Sports Science. Notice also that Psychology students at Russell Group universities are more likely to come from higher managerial and professional occupational backgrounds. Those who study Sports Science, Education and Computer Science come from different occupational backgrounds to those studying more 'high status' subjects (Table 7.3).

The stratification of elite universities, especially in terms of the ethnic and social-class make-up of the student population, has received a great deal of popular attention recently (Shepherd 2009; Blair 2005; Randall 2010; Boliver 2011). This, of course, is partly on account of the high fees that universities

Table 7.3 Subjects studied by undergraduate students from higher managerial and professional occupational backgrounds, selected subject areas

	Students from higher managerial and professional backgrounds (%)
All subjects	16
Medicine	38
Physics	26
Mathematics	24
Psychology (Russell Group)	25
Psychology (all institutions)	15
Sports Science	12
Computer Science	12
Education	9

Source: UCAS 2010.

Table 7.4   University status and student characteristics, 2010

University	Students from independent schools (%)	Students eligible for free school meals (%)
Oxford	47	0.8
Cambridge	43	0.8
Bristol	37	0.9
Exeter	28	1
Newcastle	30	1
Thames Valley	2	21
London Metropolitan	3	22
Middlesex	2	23
East London	1	23
London South Bank	2	25

Source: *The Guardian* DataBlog (2010b).

propose to charge from October 2012. However, the figures the media report are compelling. According to Freedom of Information Requests made by David Lammy (the former Labour Minister for Higher education), 89 per cent of Oxford University students come from upper- and middle-class back-grounds. The average for all British universities is 66 per cent. For Cambridge University between 1999 and 2009, one in six (16 per cent) of the highest-attaining black applicants who achieved the required grades managed to secure a place, compared with one in three (33 per cent) white applicants (*The Guardian* 2011b). There are also quite clear inequalities in participation among other universities. Table 7.4 shows the highest and lowest five ranked universities according to the percentage of students who received free school meals, as well as those who attended a school in the independent sector (*The Guardian* 2010b).

Table 7.1 to 7.4 are good examples of some of the inequalities which exist within the HE sector. The next section will consider the policy of affirma-tive action, and its use to overcome barriers to the participation of under-represented groups.

Should Under-Represented Groups be Given Priority in University Admissions?

In 1996, 43-year-old Barbara Grutter applied to the prestigious Michigan Law School in the USA. Despite having scored in the top 15 per cent of her Law School Admissions Test, the university rejected her. Barbara Grutter is white and at the time of her application, the university of Michigan, of which the Law School is a part, operated an admissions policy that prioritised applicants from under-represented groups. A consequence of these policies meant that black students with lower scores than Ms Grutter would be admitted to the Law School. Ms Grutter subsequently sued the university.

In 2003, the University of Bristol was accused of favouring state students over independent school students in its admissions process. A number of independent school students who had been predicted to achive the highest A-level grades were rejected. This led to a call from the Headmasters' and Headmistresses' Conference and the Girls' Schools Association, which represent the most prestigious independent schools, for a boycott of Bristol University (Smithers 2003). The university responded by claiming that there was no bias towards independent school students in its admissions policy and that it was against selection on any grounds other than academic potential (*The Guardian* 2003b).

When Ms Grutter applied to the University of Michigan Law School, just 8 per cent of students were black, despite the university's close proximity to the majority black city of Detroit. After a protracted legal case, in 2003 the US Supreme Court ruled that the University of Michigan was correct in accounting for race, along with other factors, in student admissions in order to achieve a racially diverse student population (University of Michigan 2003).

At this time, around 60 per cent of University of Bristol students came from the independent sector, compared with around 10 per cent nationally (Baty 2003). The admissions procedure for the University of Bristol was examined by the Independent Schools Council which cleared the university of any bias. In its defence Bristol noted that there had been more than 1,500 applications for 47 places on its English courses, for example. Of those, 1,300 potentially met the minimum-entry grades of AAB at A-level and more than 500 were predicted to achieve perfect A-level scores (Baty 2003). It was perhaps inevitable that some students would be disappointed.

The University of Michigan case represents an example of *affirmative action* which, in this instance, has been used to redress inequalities in the types of students who participate in higher education (see also Bibbings 2006; Sandel 2010). In trying to decide whether affirmative action is a just practice or not, you might wish to consider the following questions:

- Do you think that Grutter was treated unfairly?
- Grutter couldn't help being born into a white majority. So should she be rejected for something that she had no control over?
- In the USA African Americans have historically been disadvantaged. Is this sort of affirmative action a fair compensation for a legacy of slavery and racial segregation as well as strong evidence of discrimination in many areas of life even today?
- Given the advantage that attending an independent school confers on the life chances of individuals, and that students who attend these schools are over-represented in elite universities, do you think that universities in Britain should practise affirmative action and be justified in taking educational background (e.g. type of school attended) into account when allocating places?
- What do you see as the similarities and differences between these two cases? Does the US ruling on the grounds of race make it an exceptional case or would similar grounds apply to educational background, for example?

Barriers to Participation in Higher Education

The notion of *barriers* to participation is, according to Gorard et al. (2007), an attractive one because it suggests that there is an explanation for differences in participation between certain groups as well as a possible solution – the removal of the barriers. So if the cost of higher education is a barrier that prevents those from low-income groups participating then it might be argued that making HE free of charge will remove that barrier and widen participation. Indeed, a key aim of research in this area has been to determine the nature and consequences of these barriers to HE participation. Many of these barriers are considered to lie in the increased financial cost of HE (Forsyth and Furlong 2003) and in practical areas such as geographical mobility and the lack of flexible learning opportunities (Connor et al. 1999), as well as in institutional barriers such as entry requirements and timing of provision (Gorard et al. 2007). There is a vast literature describing these barriers to participation and their potential impact on the life chances of would be participants. We will look at three of the most pertinent here:

- institutional barriers: for example entry requirements, course timetabling;
- dispositional barriers: for example attitudes towards studying;
- situational barriers: for example tuition fees.

Institutional Barriers to Participation

Previous research suggests that in most contexts the most important barrier to participation in HE is prior attainment (Raffe et al. 2006; see also Broecke and Hamed 2008; Galindo-Rueda et al. 2004; NAO 2008; Chowdry et al. 2010). But given that success in education is predicated on success at the previous educational stage (Gorard et al. 2007) and as young people from less affluent social groups achieve at lower levels throughout schooling, it is perhaps unsurprising that entry to HE also is also stratified by social characteristics such as occupational class background and economic activity. There may be geographical barriers as well. According to Mangan et al. (2010) students who do not live near a high-ranking institution and who may have to live at home while at university are necessarily restricted in the choice of places to study. According to Davies et al. (2009) this is an issue which disproportionately affects those on low income.

Another example of an institutional barrier would be having an inflexible admissions process such as only recruiting at a single point (usually in September/October) in the academic year rather than recruiting students throughout the academic year. Others would include lectures that run only on weekdays from 9 am until 6 pm. This, of course, is the usual arrangement for most UK institutions. For 'traditional' students who may have recently left home and moved to study in a different part of the country, such arrangements may present little difficulty. But for those who may have to juggle caring roles, work and other responsibilities, this sort of practice may act as an additional barrier to their participation. The following extracts sum-marise these problems neatly:

> Distance is the most important thing. It's almost bound to be when you've got three young kids. (Maggie, white working-class lone mother, in Reay et al. 2005: 86)

> Because I live out in the Northeast of Glasgow, because I travel and I don't have a car either … So it kind of means that as far as things like night life goes and being part of the student life I don't have anything to do with that really, I am more involved with people from work [the Co-op shop] and stuff who aren't basically students. You feel you are missing out on student life quite a lot by not being out there. (HE student, in Forsyth and Furlong 2000: 37)

Dispositional Barriers to Participation

A concern of some participants that HE might not be for 'people like them' has been a key focus of research into barriers to participation. These dispo-sitional factors include a reluctance to apply to an elite university because of a fear of not fitting in (for example, Forsyth and Furlong 2003; Reay et al. 2005) or a lack of knowledge about what university life may be like, particularly among students who have been away from formal education for a prolonged period of time. Another important factor can be a difficulty in adapting to the culture of HE. This can result in a lack of motivation and poorer attitudes to learning, which might be one – but certainly not the only – reason why some students may drop out (Gorard et al. 2007). For example, according to research by Cooke et al. (2004) students from lower socioeconomic backgrounds engage in fewer non-academic activities (e.g. sport clubs or societies) and spend less time socialising compared to those who are more 'advantaged'. This might be related to the fact that these stu-dents were more likely to be in paid employment while studying compared to their more advantaged peers:

> I don't see the point in spending my time with people who are not going to be able to relate to me and I'm not going to be able to relate to them. We are from different worlds, so I think I've had enough of that in my life … I don't want to feel as if I have to pretend to be someone I'm not. (Janice, black working-class lone parent, in Reay et al. 2005: 94)

Situational Barriers to Participation

A key situational barrier to participation would be the increasing financial cost of study, a topic that is, of course, of particular interest at the moment. In October 2010 Lord Browne, the former head of British Petroleum, pre-sented his long-awaited report into higher education funding (BIS 2010d). The key recommendation of the Browne Report was a lifting of the cap on university tuition fees from its current rate of £3,290 per year to a maximum amount of £9,000 from September 2012. Students would not be required to pay this amount 'up front' but would be loaned the funds from the government and expected to start their repayments once they reached a threshold income of £21,000 (BIS 2010a). The recommendations of the Browne Report coincided with the government's announcement that the funding it provides for higher education, which in effect subsidies the fees that students are currently paying, would be reduced from £7.1 billion to £4.2 billion by 2014/15. This represents a 40 per cent, or £2.9 billion, reduction. Although the government will continue to fund teaching for Science, Technology, Engineering and Mathematics (STEM) subjects this will not be the case for other subject areas (BIS 2010b).

The recommendation that students pay a proportion of the costs of their tuition is not new: it was mentioned by Robbins (Committee on Higher Education, 1963, para, 641–7) and addressed more fully by Dearing (NCIHE 1997). However, the likelihood of a trebling of fees represents a huge change in the nature of HE, particularly in England. Note that in the other home nations there are different arrangements for funding HE. In Wales, for example, at the time of writing, any increases to the costs of tuition for Welsh-domiciled students would be met by the Welsh assembly government (BBC 2010g). Although the government has asserted that universities would only be able to charge the maximum amount of £9,000 in 'exceptional cases' and be subject to 'tougher conditions on widening participation and fair access' (BIS 2010c), the majority of universities propose setting their fees at £9,000 (BBC 2011c).

One of the fundamental concerns of those who oppose tuition fees is that they will deter already under-represented groups from participating (Chowdry 2010; OECD 2011b). But the impact of fees on participation is unclear. According to research by Callender and Jackson (2008) financial issues provide more of a constraint on participation for lower-social-class students in comparison with those from other social groups. However, the data from UCAS does not show any appreciable difference in patterns of applications following the introduction of tuition fees of around £3,000 per year and there is also limited evidence that this has reduced the relative HE participation rate of poorer students (Chowdry et al. 2010).

Time will tell what the effect of tuition fees on the sector will be but the issue of fees raises important questions about who should fund higher education. Part of Deputy Prime Minister Nick Clegg's reasons for supporting the restructuring of the fees system is because he argues that it will benefit graduates on low incomes: those whose salary started at £21,000 and rose to £27,000 after 20 years would find themselves having to pay a relatively low contribution (possibly around £7 a month) to the costs of their study (BBC 2010h), while those students who earn high wages will be expected to pay back the costs of the education that enabled them to command such high salaries. Opponents of fees argue that they will deter students from the poorest families – often the most debt averse – from applying, while having no impact on the very wealthiest who are likely to be accustomed to paying upwards of £9,000 in fees for a top independent school place anyhow.

Reflection: What is the fairest way to fund higher education?

There are many different ways in which you might debate this topic. This example considers whether society benefits from having a university-educated population and should therefore shoulder the cost.

One perspective is that having a highly educated workforce benefits the whole of society. Everyone benefits from having university educated doctors, lawyers, engineers and so on and therefore it is fair that society supports those individuals who have the ability and/or desire to pursue these careers. It would be unfair for them to incur large personal debt in order to undertake their studies.

An alternative point of view is given by Brian whose comment on a BBC notice board read:

> It simply isn't fair that bin men and postmen pay for students to study media studies through their taxes. It is surely fair for those students to pay, when their salary allows it in the future, for their own education. (Written by Brian in London at 13: 20, BBC 2010g)

This view argues that although doctors and others may benefit society in their work, they already reap large personal reward in the form of enhanced salaries and status in society and therefore it is only fair that they contribute to some of the cost of this. Saying that society should fund this is, for some, akin to the argument that lowering taxes for the rich encourages them to spend more which in turn creates work for the poor. What are your views on this?

Do We Need a System of Mass Higher Education?

Having considered the implications of a mass higher education system, it is perhaps inevitable that we ask ourselves whether it really is necessary that 50 per cent of young people should have some form of higher education.

In his classic 1979 book *The Diploma Disease* (reprinted in 1997), Ronald Dore wrote of both an escalation and inflation in the qualifications that individuals were seeking to accrue. By this he meant both a rise in the number of qualifications required for any particular job and a subsequent fall in the job-getting value of a particular qualification. This, he argues, will lead to people 'staying on in school longer than either their intrinsic person-development benefits from learning or their need to learn something occupationally useful would justify' (1997: ix). His classic example was that of a librarian who at the beginning of the twentieth century had only to have a 'love of books and the capacity to advise the managers as to purchases and the inquirers as to suitable works' (p. 23). By the 1930s a school certificate was considered to be a 'useful possession' for a librarian but by the 1950s it was a minimum requirement. By the 1970s a librarian required at least two A-levels and today advertisements for librarians frequently require at least an undergraduate degree and often a postgraduate qualification as well. Thus it is not necessarily the case that librarians have to be educated to Masters level in order to do their job effectively (although some might argue that the increasingly technical nature of their work requires some additional training). But the point that Dore makes is that the increased need for additional qualifications has come about because we use qualifications to select people for jobs. This means that we have a situation where there is pressure for learners to gain qualifications in order to *get* a job rather than to gain qualifications in order to be able to *do* a job.

We see this situation quite clearly with the current move to a mass system of higher education. In the field of Education it is not an unreasonable expectation for an Education graduate to seek employment as a teaching assistant, possibly as preparation for a PGCE. The minimum requirements for a teaching assistant have traditionally been set below degree level and so is it the case that an Education Studies graduate is overqualified for this role?

According to Alison Wolf, who chaired the recent review into vocational education and training: 'It is demonstrably the case that the UK economy ... does not "need" as many graduates as it currently produces, in the sense that many jobs are now done by graduates which were once done quite satisfactorily by people who had not gone to university' (Wolf 2008a: 38). Wolf's assertion is supported by recent work by Chevalier and Lindley (2009) who argue that since the recent expansion of HE the probability of graduates being 'overeducated' for their job has doubled. They suggest that 11 to 15 per cent of graduates are in jobs that do not require graduate skills and as a consequence will earn less money than had they occupied jobs which pay at graduate rates. This loss of income can eliminate any financial benefit which might be accrued from attending university: a situation which will of course have particular consequences given recent increases in tuition fees.

Summary

Over the last twenty years or so, we have gradually been moving towards a system of mass higher education in the UK. But even though more people than ever before are receiving a university education does it mean that our HE system is more equitable? Inequalities in HE participation persist. They are evident in much the same way as the other educational and social inequalities that we have explored in this book: in terms of sex, age, parental social class, parental education, type of school attended, housing tenure, health, family structure and so on. It is certainly the case that a university education is now open to more people who might never previously have thought about attending, but we need to ask serious questions about the type of university experience that they have. Evidence suggests that despite increased access to HE, universities are still internally stratified according to social characteristics based largely on class: students who attended the elite independent schools still command a disproportionate share of the places on the elite courses at the elite universities. But does this matter? Widening access to HE means that many, many people who would otherwise not have gone to university now have the opportunity to attend. Perhaps it does not matter that they do not study Medicine at Cambridge – they have still had the opportunity to study at university level and have been exposed to the benefits that such an education can accrue.

 Reflection

Let us consider access to HE from the perspective of our three principles of justice: equality, need and merit.

Justice as equality would argue that a university education should be open to everyone who wants it and minimum qualifications should be all that are required. This is similar to the US model of HE where admissions rates for some institutions can be very liberal. For example, in 2009/10 Arizona State University, the largest research-led university in the US, offered places to 91 per cent of its 28,304 undergraduate applicants. But of course students have to pay rather a lot for this privilege: annual tuition fees for students who are from Arizona in 2010/11 were around £5,000 (NCES 2011), although admittedly this is less than many UK students will be paying in 2012.

Can you develop your own arguments for increasing, or widening, participation in HE according to the principles of need and of merit?

Notes

1. Polytechnics were tertiary-level institutions that differed from universities in that their focus was traditionally on vocational programmes. The 1992 Further and Higher Education Act abolished the distinction between polytechnics and universities.
2. Further information on the different categories of UK higher education institutions can be found at: http://www.eurydice.org.

Further reading

Furlong, A. and Cartmel, F. (2009) *Higher education and Social Justice*. Open University Press.

Gorard, S., Adnett, N., May, H., Slack, K., Smith, E. and Thomas, L. (2007) *Overcoming the Barriers to Higher Education*. Stoke-on-Trent: Trentham Books.

Reay, D., David, M. and Ball, S. (2005) *Degrees of Choice: Social Class, Race, Gender in Higher Education*. Stoke-on-Trent: Trentham Books.

Social justice and the learning society

A great deal of the discussion around the expansion of the education system in the UK and the so-called 'knowledge economy' that it seeks to service has focused on higher education. But not everyone goes to university. To quote from Alison Wolf's book *Does Education Matter?* 'the poor don't go to university. The children of the middle classes do' (Wolf 2000: 253). In fact recent estimates suggest that around 11 per cent of 16–24 year olds in the UK have no formal educational qualifications at all (DfE 2010h). In an oversaturated graduate market (Hankinson 2010) where many current graduates are over-qualified for their current job, what opportunities are there for young people who have neither the inclination nor the resources (either intellectual or financial) to continue in education after the age of 16? This chapter will focus on those at risk of being left behind in the march towards a system of 'mass' higher education. One of the key reasons behind attempts to increase participation in post-compulsory education and training has been the need to produce a skilled and technically competent workforce. Here we also look at two additional aspects of our apparent skills deficit, first, those young people who do not engage in education, employment and training; and secondly, the large group of older people who left compulsory education and have not engaged in education and training since.

A lost generation? Coming of Age During a Recession

With the new millennium came a new description for the disengaged, disaffected and unemployed: the NEET (OfES 2000; Social Exclusion Unit 1999). As the newspaper headlines below indicate, for many young people being a NEET (not in education, employment or training) can present not only a personal challenge but also a serious 'social and political public problem'.

'The lost generation: surge in joblessness hits young'. (*Guardian*, August 2009)

'Now Britain is the NEET capital of Western Europe ...' (*Daily Mail*, January 2011)

'Top mandarin: 15% of NEETs die within 10 years'. (*TES*, August 2009)

'Society grapples with infestation of NEETs'. (*Western Mail*, March 2005)

It is estimated that NEETs cost the taxpayer nearly £12 billion in benefit payments and tax loss (Coles et al. 2010: 5).

In the 1980s changes to the way in which unemployment was measured in the UK meant that young people under the age of 18 were no longer counted in the unemployment figures. The 1988 Social Security Act removed unemployment benefit for the under-18s resulting in around 120,000 young people being deleted from the unemployment record (Levitas 1996). As official records no longer recognised youth unemployment, researchers started to look for new ways of estimating the vulnerability of young people who were not engaged in work or training (Furlong 2006). Researchers working in South Wales in the early 1990s used the term 'status zerO' (Rees et al. 1996) to describe those young people who had left school with no formal qualifications and often had criminal records (Williamson 2004). Attempts to clarify the composition of this group led to the formal designation of 'NEET' to describe those young people who left school at an early age and had not engaged with work, education or training (Social Exclusion Unit 1999). Although in many ways this is a pejorative, perhaps even an ill-conceived, term which disguises the complexity and heterogeneity of this group (Furlong 2006; Hansard 2010b; LSN 2009), the NEET has become synanymous with a disadvantaged lost generation – the core of 'broken Britain' who are held responsible for a range of social ills: teenage pregnancy, crime, anti-social behaviour and drug abuse (Prince's Trust 2010a, 2011).

Although the recent recession has meant that unemployment figures have risen across all age groups, young people now make up 38 per cent of the 2.5 million people of working age who are unemployed (Potton 2010). As you can see from Figure 8.1, the proportion of young people who are either classed as unemployed or NEET tends to be higher than the unemployment level of the general working-age population. So in 2009 almost 20 per cent of young people aged 16–24 were out of work.

Recent data on unemployment suggests that young people have been particularly badly affected by the recent recession and downturn in the global economy (Ha et al. 2010; Wolf 2011). In summer 2010, over 1 million people aged 16–24 were not in any form of employment, education or training. This is equivalent to 17 per cent of the whole age group and is a rise of almost 150,000 over the figures for the same time of year in 2005 (DfE 2010h). Among the 16–19 age group the number of young people who are NEET is usually estimated to be around 10 per cent but frequently a further six to seven per cent of young people are unaccounted for and estimates suggest that the figure might be as high as 17–20 per cent in some London boroughs (LSN 2009).

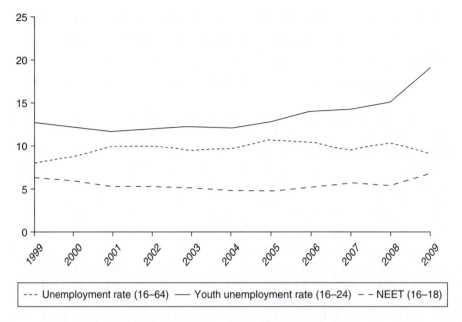

Figure 8.1 Unemployment rates, youth and general population

Source: Office for National Statistics (2010b), Eurostat (2010a), DfE (2010h).

Writing in the Irish context, Smyth and McCoy (2009) show that even in times of economic prosperity, those who leave school with few formal qualifications are likely to experience significant problems in securing paid employment. This is a disadvantage which continues well into adulthood. And the prospects for those leaving school with little or no formal qualifications at a time of recession are arguably even bleaker.

Although the term may have originated in the UK, the NEET is not an exclusively British phenomenon. For example, in Japan, a country often regarded by Western commentators and politicians to be an academic and industrial success story, NEETs are considered to be a 'significant social problem' (*Japan Times* 2009; Genda 2007). Indeed high levels of youth unemployment and disengagement from education persist in many developed nations, with a recent report published by the International Labour Organisation (ILO 2010) suggesting that globally around 13 per cent of 15–24 year olds are economically inactive. Table 8.1 shows the percentage of 18–24 year olds who are NEET in eight EU countries. Notice the comparatively high number of NEETs in Spain, Italy and Ireland.

Table 8.1 NEETs aged 18–24, selected EU countries 2009 (%)

All EU	Germany	Finland	Sweden	France	UK	Italy	Spain	Ireland
16.0	11.9	12.9	13.1	16.4	17.1	22.4	22.6	23.1

Source: Eurostat (2010b).

The Education Maintenance Allowance

In October 2010 the Coalition government announced plans to abolish the Education Maintenance Allowance (EMA). The plans provoked a huge outcry and swelled the ranks of those who demonstrated against the government's proposed changes to funding of further and higher education in England (BBC 2010h). Central to the protesters' concerns were the claims that EMAs ensured more equitable access to post-compulsory education and training for young people from the poorest homes and that scrapping the allowance would further increase inequalities in participation in post-compulsory education and training and so potentially contribute to the number of young people who are NEET.

EMAs were introduced in 2004 to provide financial support for students from low-income families. They consist of a means-tested weekly payment of up to £30 for young people studying in full-time education or training. It is estimated that around 650,000 16–19 year olds were in receipt of EMA, at a cost to the treasury of over £560 million a year (DfE 2011g). In its place the government proposed to offer more 'targeted' funds to be distributed by individual schools and colleges at their discretion. In explaining their decision to remove the EMA, the government has drawn heavily upon research evidence from a study into the barriers to participation in post-16 education and training and in particular the study's conclusion that 'only 12% of young people overall receiving an EMA believe that they would not have participated in the courses they are doing if they had not received an EMA' (Spielhofer et al. 2010: 45; see also DfE 2011g). The main evidence for this study was derived from a survey of 2,029 young people who completed Year 11 in either 2008 or 2009 and which was conducted between August and October 2009. Arguably for the young people who finished Year 11 in 2009, and whose exact numbers are unclear from the report, this is very early in their post-16 career for them to be forming an accurate opinion about any barriers that they might face. This study's findings contradict those from another piece of research undertaken by the Institute for Fiscal Studies which suggests that the EMA 'significantly raised the stay-on rates past the age of 16' (Dearden et al. 2009: 848), especially for those with lower levels of prior attainment. Similarly, research carried out on behalf of the Centre for British Teachers also concluded that the EMA has been successful in increasing participation among 16 and 17 year olds, particularly among low-attaining students, those from single parent households and those from certain ethnic minority groups (Fletcher 2009).

So which evidence should we believe? I have included links to different perspectives on the EMA on the website that accompanies this book. Have a look and decide for yourself.

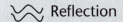 Reflection

As you can see from the above, the evidence either supporting or contradicting the government's decision to scrap the EMA can be complex.

(Continued)

(Continued)

Indeed, as the two extracts below indicate, it is also an issue which divides those who are directly affected by the plans:

'The cuts announced in the spending review seem to be hitting people who are already having a tough time the hardest. My mum died when I was seven, so my dad is the only wage earner in our household. He lost his job two years ago, so money is really tight and I rely on the EMA to cover my travel costs from Basingstoke to college in Winchester every day. It's only an 18-minute journey, but it costs me over £350 a term in train fares. And now I hear we're also going to have to weather a 3% rise in rail fares. I do wonder if the government is putting up tuition fees because it wants to discourage young people from going to university and set their sights a bit lower. I still want to go to university, because I want to be a barrister, and I need a degree for that, but the prospect of running up over £40k of debt is depressing.'

A-level student at Peter Symonds, a sixth form college, Winchester, Hampshire

'I'm not surprised to hear the EMA is being abolished, because it is so open to abuse. While I realise it's vital for some students, a lot of young people round here could do without it. I often hear people saying they're waiting for their weekly payment so they can go shopping, to the cinema or out for lunch. I get the EMA, but I don't really need the money. I'm eligible because I live with my mum, who earns less than £16,000 a year. My dad earns loads more, but that isn't taken into account. I get my EMA transferred straight into a savings account for university.'

(A-level student at Bayhouse School and Sixth Form, Gosport, Hampshire)

Extracts taken from *The Guardian* newspaper, 25 October 2010
(cited in Murray 2010)

'Lonely, Rejected, Lost, Desperate': a Closer Look at the NEETs

Notwithstanding the diversity of the NEET group, they tend to have several characteristics in common. Research suggests that NEETs tend to come from less advantaged economic and educational backgrounds, they tend to have lower academic qualifications, have high levels of truancy or absenteeism from school, less favourable attitudes to school and, for girls, are often characterised by early motherhood (DfES 2000; Bynner and Parsons 2002, Raffe 2003; Croll 2009; Cusworth et al. 2009). However, the majority of NEETs 'do not conform to the stereotype of the workshy and feckless' and instead have similar aspirations to those of other young people (LSN 2009: 1). Being NEET is also very transient – young people are unlikely to remain NEET for long and often embark on routes which move them into and out of various types of employment and training (Wolf 2008b).

For some the consequences of being NEET in early adulthood are a life of poverty, poor health and social exclusion. In 2011 the Prince's Trust published its third Youth Index survey which measured the happiness and well-being of young people in Britain today, as well as asking them about their hopes for the future (Prince's Trust 2011). Undertaken in conjunction with the on-line market research company YouGov, the survey questioned 2,170 young people aged 16–25 (16 per cent of whom reported they were NEET). The findings show that young people who are NEET tend to be less happy and confident than their peers. They are more likely to feel that their life lacks direction, suffer episodes of poor mental health and think that they have nothing to look forward to. This research supports a number of studies undertaken over the last decade or so which have looked at the experiences of young disengaged young people who are often at the point of moving between education and work. One thing many of these studies have in common is that they reach the conclusion that the 'world is a hard place to go nowhere in' (Bynner et al. 1997: 136).

However, disengaged and disaffected youth are not a new phenomenon: problematic transitions from school to work are characteristic of many generations (Willis 1977; Williamson 2004). For example, Bynner and Parsons' work with the 1970 British Cohort Study shows that those born in 1970 faced exceptional difficulties in making a successful transition to work:

> In the context of a disappearing youth labour market, and considerable uncertainty about the means of maximizing job opportunities in the future, these young people faced the choice of whether to stay on in education or leave, and if they left, whether to take any job or training scheme on offer or wait for something better to turn up. (Bynner and Parsons, 2002: 303)

More recently, there is Fran Abrams' account of young people's successful, and more frequently less successful, transitions to the workforce. Studies such as Abrams' demonstrate very clearly the challenges that are faced by marginalised young people today who are often brought up in marginalised communities (Abrams 2010). Ainley and Allen's 2010 book *Lost Generation? New Strategies for Youth and Education* provides similar accounts.

Reducing the Numbers of Young People Who are Neet?

Over the last decade or so there have been a number of policy initiatives whose aim has been to tackle the problem of youth unemployment (Maguire and Thompson 2007). Central to these programmes is the need for learning providers, however they are organised, to produce more and more young people with the employability skills that industry and business demands (see, for example, UKCES 2009). The New Deal for Young People, Train to Gain, the Connexions service, the Future Jobs fund and the National Apprenticeship scheme are just some examples of schemes aimed at increasing the skills and employment opportunities of young people. For some researchers this emphasis on vocational education for the disadvantaged and the unemployed is problematic, and does little to improve the vocational–academic curriculum divide which has long been a feature of education in this country: 'It is extraordinary to believe that targeting vocational education at our lowest achieving fourteen year olds will solve skill shortages' (Wolf 2000: 252).

The difference in esteem between vocational and academic qualifications is a long-standing challenge to the education system in this country. For decades the 'gold standard' that is the A-level has been the gateway qualification to higher education and has proven itself to be remarkably resistant to any tinkering. According to the recent review into vocational education and training undertaken by Alison Wolf (2011), while many young people in England experience high-quality vocational education which leads successfully into employment or higher education, most do not. In fact many English low-level vocational qualifications, notably NVQ Levels 1 and 2, currently have little to no apparent labour market value – in other words they are of little or no benefit in helping the student get a job. The Wolf Review estimates that among 16–19 year olds, at least 350,000 get little to no benefit from the post-16 education system (Wolf 2011).

In England the school participation age will be raised from 16 to 17 in 2013 and to 18 by 2015 (DCSF 2007). This will naturally mean that young people intending to leave education and training at 16 and go directly into employment will no longer be able to do so. Instead they will have three options: to remain in full-time education in school or college, to undertake work-based training such as an apprenticeship, or to study part-time if they are employed for more than 20 hours per week. This will have huge consequences for the post-compulsory training sector which will have to accommodate the many thousands of possibly reluctant learners who will need to remain in some form of education or training until the age of 18. This is an issue we consider next.

Raising the School Leaving Age and Social Justice

The raising of the school leaving age to 18 in 2015 presents an interesting case study for those interested in issues of social justice in education (see Box 8.1). It is therefore worth considering some of the arguments that are presented for and against the plans.

In the Foreword to the document *Raising Expectations: Staying in Education and Training Post-16*, Ed Balls, the former Labour Secretary of State for

Children, Schools and Families, outlines the government's rationale for raising the participation age to 18:

> The demands of the economy, and our ambition for social justice, mean that we must do more. We need excellence in education and training not just for some but for all young people. (DCSF 2007: 1)

The argument that all young people, regardless of background, should have the same opportunity to remain in education is a powerful one. The report points to the financial advantages for individuals who remain in education beyond the age of 16, a benefit that it argues can add around £100,000 to the lifetime earnings for those who achieve five A*–C grades at GCSE. There are also the social advantages: fewer instances of teenage pregnancy, anti-social behaviour and criminality. And, of course, there are the economic benefits to the country of having a well educated and technically competent workforce. Given the potentially devastating consequences of life as a 'NEET', this increased focus on the provision of education and training opportunities for those who traditionally do not participate is arguably laudable and could have advantages in improving social justice and opportunities. As the Leitch Review of Skills argues: 'Achieving world class skills is *the* key to achieving economic success and social justice in the new global economy' (Leitch Review of Skills 2006: 9).

However, there is a counter-argument to these plans, the key thrust of which is that the very young people who will be forced to remain in education are those who have been the least successful in school and arguably many will be those whom the education system has failed. Opponents argue that this new 'duty' on young people to remain in training until the age of 18 is an affront to personal freedom and amounts to little more than 'coercing' them to remain in education to study for meaningless qualifications and serves simply to delay their unsuccessful transition into the labour market. A likely outcome of this is that large numbers of 'forced participants' will negatively affect the learning environment and will serve to 'depress' the youth labour market (Wolf 2008b). As we discussed earlier one of the main reasons why the education participation age will be increased to 18 is economic and reflects the need to 'up-skill' the British workforce in order to enable to country to compete more effectively in the global economy. According to Simmons (2010: 422), however, this premise is both 'misleading' and 'questionable'. He maintains that the demand for high-level knowledge and skills is 'exaggerated' and instead 'that low-skilled work, usually poorly paid and often transitory in nature, is increasingly the reality of the UK economy' (p. 430). Wolf (2008b) agrees and predicts that the consequences of increased participation will be more young people studying for low-value qualifications which may have little resemblance to the skills needed for employment. She concludes that it 'hardly sounds like a recipe for economic transformation and social justice that the Government has been predicting' (p. 17).

Box 8.1 Raising the school leaving age

One argument against raising the school leaving age is presented below. It is adapted from a blog comment posted in the *Times Educational Supplement* on 17 December 2007 by the teacher and author Daniel Ken.

Jodie is a bright and articulate sixteen year-old; a natural leader, she has a large circle of friends. In class, however, she is a nightmare; argumentative, disruptive and, when it suits her, prone to violence. Sustained poor behaviour has meant that she has been regularly excluded from school since the age of eight.

But she has qualities in abundance; she's quick-witted, engaging and is a great communicator. If I were asked, I'd point her in the direction of a career where she has to take responsibility, take decisions and work hard. I'd suggest a job where her natural authority and likeability is given a chance to shine; where her volatility could be focussed into action. A paramedic, maybe or a police officer. I think, once she's in the adult world, with adult expectations and adult responsibilities, she'll do fine. I think the world of work is the best thing that can happen to Jodie and I look forward to meeting her in ten or fifteen years' time; I think she'll have flourished.

But forcing Jodie to stay in full-time education would not help her. Nor would it address her terrible behaviour. And it would be extremely detrimental to the learning of every other student in the class. Keeping kids like Jodie in the classroom until they're eighteen, would simply entrench the most negative aspects of their personality. No matter that the sort of kids who become NEETs are the very kids for whom the previous eleven years of education has failed, the Government will push on regardless with their plans and once again teachers will be forced to fulfil a hybrid role of educator, social worker and police officer.

In your opinion, is raising the school leaving age the right thing to do in order to address youth unemployment? If not, then what alternatives might there be?

The Need to Improve Our Skills

Our nation's skills are not world class and we run the risk that this will undermine the UK's long-term prosperity … without increased skills we would condem ourselves to a lingering decline in competitiveness, diminishing economic growth and a bleaker future for all. (Leitch Review of Skills 2006: 1)

The imperative to improve a nation's skills base and as a consequence increase productivity, employment and economic competitiveness is apparent in much of the policy discourse around post-compulsory education and training in the UK as well as in other developed nations (Leitch Review of Skills 2006 and National Academy of Sciences 2007). Indeed, the idea that 'education can make us all richer' (Wolf 2008a: 37) has been the primary driver behind UK education policy for over three decades. The basis for such an assertion is as follows: people who earn the most money tend to be those who hold the highest educational qualifications and so if everyone were to be educated to the same high level, they would all earn a similarly large amount of money. This would in turn benefit the country and its global economic competitiveness. Or put more bluntly: 'Give the uneducated education … and the problems of social exclusion will be solved' (Wolf 2000: 251). Such sentiments are not new, as the former Prime Minister James Callaghan argued in his Ruskin College speech in 1976:

> There is no virtue in producing socially well-adjusted members of society who are unemployed because they do not have the skills. (Reprinted in *The Guardian* 2001b)

However, the evidence that a good education system necessarily equates to a successful economy is according to Wolf 'preposterously thin'. Wolf (2000) argues that although having high-quality, universal primary- and secondary-level education in which all children have equal opportunity to develop a core set of skills is the bedrock of a modern society, the same cannot be said for education at the tertiary level – that is in further and higher education. Of course a country needs to produce the highly qualified engineers and technicians that modern society depends upon. The issue is whether we need to feed an expanding education sector for its own sake, where its graduates will take the jobs that were previously taken by non-graduates. That the more qualified do better in the labour market is only partially due to the level of education that they have received: education is a positional good; its benefit to some extent lies in possessing something (i.e. a level of qualification) that few others have. The more people that have a particular qualification – the GCSE grade G is a good example of this – the less value that qualification carries. You can read more of this argument in Ronald Dore's book *The Diploma Disease* (1997).

Despite the above concerns about educational and training provision for the young, NEETs comprise a relatively small part (around 10 per cent) of the potential workforce. According to figures provided by the Coalition government around 80 per cent of the 2020 workforce has already left compulsory education (BIS 2010a). With almost one third of working age adults in England not holding the equivalent of an A*–C grade at GCSE (Data Service 2009) and a quarter of Scottish adults lacking the literacy skills acceptable for a modern economy (St Clair et al. 2010) it is perhaps unsurprising that efforts at the school level will not be enough to address our apparent skills deficit. This brings us to the second great challenge of post-compulsory education and training: lifelong learning.

Creating a Learning Society?

A learning society is one in which:

> All citizens acquire a high quality general education, appropriate vocational training and a job … while continuing to participate in education and training throughout their lives. (Coffield 1998)

Apart from the economic motivations discussed above, there is an additional reason why the ideal of a learning society is important. This is the hope that because education and its rewards are unevenly distributed in

Table 8.2 Participation in formal and/or informal learning, selected OECD countries

	Below upper secondary education[a] (%)	Upper secondary education[b] (%)	Tertiary education[c] (%)	All levels of education (%)
Australia	23	38	53	38
Canada	22	36	57	47
Finland	35	52	73	55
France	19	34	57	35
Germany	20	45	63	45
Spain	17	35	51	31
Sweden	56	72	90	73
UK	33	53	63	49
USA	23	37	63	49
OECD av.	22	40	60	41

[a]Left school at around age
[b]Left education at around age
[c]Attended higher education

Indicator A5: How many adults participate in education and learning? 2007 education at a Glance (OECD 2010e).

Source: OECD 2010, LSO network special data collection, Adult Learning Working Group.

Britain, widening participation will help increase social justice and help share the benefits of education more fairly among the population (Gorard and Rees 2002). Therefore a successful learning society would be one in which everyone obtains high-quality general education leading to a comprehensive post-school education and training system where everyone has access to suitable opportunities for lifelong learning (Coffield 1998).

Adult skills shortages are not just an issue for the UK (OECD 2003). As the figures in Table 8.2 show, levels of participation in adult education vary across OECD countries. For most of the countries shown here, adults with the lowest educational qualifications are less likely to participate in any sort of formal or informal learning. Informal learning might involve teaching yourself to do something at home, such as learning a language, carpentry or car maintenance. More formal learning might involve taking a part-time evening course at a local college.

In Spain, for example only 17 per cent of those who left school at around the age of 16 continued to learn. An exception to these patterns is Sweden where lifelong learning appears to be much more prevalent. In the UK, participation rates are slightly higher than the OECD average, with almost two-thirds of those who left school at the age of 18 continuing to undertake some type of learning, either formal or informal.

 Reflection

Table 8.2 appears to show that those who engage in education for the least amount of time are also those who are less likely to be adult learners. What does this tell us about the likely effectiveness of initiatives to encourage more low-skilled workers to become lifelong learners?

So who are the adult learners? As Table 8.2 shows, they tend to be the more highly educated. They also tend to be younger and, in the UK at least, they are slightly more likely to be female. Gorard and Rees (2002) also emphasise the importance of learner identities in determining whether or not adults engage in education and training. As you can see from the following extract the notion that such opportunities are 'not for the likes of me' can often act as an important barrier to involvement:

> You said about education, about getting qualifications ... I might fall into some-thing that I would really love ... but you asked me about getting education ... which I think would be a foolish thing for me to do really ... It's a waste of time as far as I'm concerned. (Respondent in Gorard and Rees 2002: 116)

Over the last fifteen years or so, there have been numerous policies and initiatives whose aim has been to increase the numbers of adults who engage in formal and informal learning activities. Although Wolf et al. (2006) provide some evidence that 'low-skilled individuals are achieving new qualifications at higher levels than before', when they examine the effect of such qualifications on how much people earn 'very little positive impact can be found' (p. 552). One important area of development has involved promoting the wider use of digital technology and in particular the idea that technology can be used to make 'the process of education fairer, more equal and more just' (Selwyn 2011: 92). We look briefly at this in the next section.

Overcoming the Digital Divide

Through huge investment in ICT and other digital technologies the aim has been to build a technology-based learning society with the social and economic benefits that this will accrue. In many ways the increasing popularity of digital technologies make this a potentially rich area for focusing attention on encouraging returning learners. For example, in 2010, nearly three-quarters of all UK households had access to the Internet, the majority of whom used it to send and receive emails (ONS 2010c), with social networking sites such as Facebook, Twitter and MySpace also becoming hugely popular. However, the key issue here is to separate out access to digital technologies from how people choose to use them. In 2010 over 17.4 million adults used the Internet to watch television or listen to the radio – almost three times as many as in 2006 – whereas only around a third say they use the Internet for learning (ONS 2010c; see also White 2012).

One example of a recent initiative is the Home Access scheme. Launched in January 2010 its purpose is to help low-income families, who currently lack access to a computer and/or the Internet, to get online at home to support learning. One aim of schemes like this is to provide everyone with an equal opportunity to engage in on-line learning, in this case through the provision of computers. Another purpose of schemes such as this is to use ICTs to help reduce the barriers to participation and enable learners to have more control over their education (Selwyn 2011).

So what evidence is there that ICTs encourage reluctant learners to re-engage in education and in doing so help realise the aims of a learning society? Selwyn et al.'s (2005) study of 1,001 adults goes some way to helping us answer this question. They identified the following factors as most likely to determine whether or not an individual used ICT for learning:

- When they were born: younger people were more likely to use ICTs for learning.
- Where they live: those who lived in the most economically disadvantaged areas were less likely to use ICTs for learning.
- Their father's occupation: this was one of the key determinants of participation. Participants whose fathers had held professional jobs and who had remained in education were more likely to engage in lifelong learning. The link with mother's occupation was less strong, probably because stay-at-home mothers might also come from wealthier households.
- Their level of education: perhaps unsurprisingly people who had remained in education beyond the compulsory phase were also more likely to continue to learn.

They conclude that ICTs present no 'universal solution' (p. 192) to non-participation, rather the use of ICTs merely reflects previous learning behaviours and does not appear to make people more likely to participate in learning. So when people do use computers, as we have seen with increased Internet use in the UK, it is not for education and learning. Indeed, there is little or no evidence that 'computers create learning where there was none previously' (p. 121). More recent work by White (2012) that used large-scale national data on adult participation in learning over a ten-year period reached a similar conclusion.

Summary

Despite a large increase in the number of young people remaining in education or training beyond the age of 18, it is important to remember that not everyone goes to university. The expansion of the HE sector has served, if anything, to expose deep inequalities for those who are left behind. In England today there are nearly 1 million young people aged between 16 and 24 who are not in any form of education, employment or training. In other words, they are NEET. Regardless of the cost to the taxpayer in benefit payments and other support, being NEET comes at much personal cost in terms of family relationships, health, well-being and of course simply having a future to look forward to. In 2015 the school leaving age will be raised from 16 to 18 and all young people will be expected to engage in more extended periods of education or training. The consequence of this, according to some researchers, is that those who may never have fully engaged in education will now be expected to continue to study or train, often in low-quality training with limited employment prospects. As well as wishing to reduce the numbers of NEETs a second focus of the post-compulsory learning agenda has been to encourage more adults to participate in formal or informal education or training. In attempting to create a learning society where people continue to engage in some form of learning throughout their lives, the government has invested greatly in schemes such as Learn Direct and in particular has encouraged the more widespread use of ICTs. While this has meant that more adults may be embarking upon adult learning schemes, the success of such schemes in improving entry to the workforce is doubtful. Indeed, researchers have shown that the people who benefit from increased learning provision are those who would engage in education or training anyway while the most vulnerable and marginalised slip further behind.

 Reflection

According to Simmons (2010: 434) 'Rather than increasing social justice, extending the age of compulsory participation may simply serve to increase social class inequalities.' This could lead to a system where prestigious schools ofter Pre-U and Baccalaureate qualifications while those in the 'middle' are pushed towards new vocational-based diplomas, leaving low-level and basic skills qualifications for the 'disaffected, the resistant and other challenged sections of society' (p. 435; see also Ainley and Allen 2010).

To what extent do you think this is a realistic concern? What do you see as being the key challenges for creating a learning society?

Further reading

Abrams, F. (2010) *Learning to Fail: How Society Lets Young People Down*. London: Routledge.

Gorard, S. and Rees, G. (2002) *Creating a Learning Society*? Bristol: Policy Press.

Williamson, H. (2004) *The Milltown Boys Revisited*. Oxford: Berg.

Concluding comments

Educational equity is a moral imperative for a society in which education is a crucial determinant of life chances.

(Levin 2009)

This book has considered the extent to which educational inequalities persist across the life-course from early childhood through to the experiences that different groups of pupils have in an increasingly diverse public school system and into a post-compulsory education and training sector.

The first chapter began with a very basic introduction to some of the key questions we might ask ourselves when deciding how to distribute educational goods (or resources) fairly. We looked at three main principles of fairness: justice as equality, justice as need and justice as desert. One conclusion that we drew from this discussion was that it was difficult to have just one principle of justice that we could apply to all circumstances. In Chapter 2 we read that the inequalities we concern ourselves with in the field of education are also present in wider society: in the different types of neighbourhoods where people live, in how much money they earn, in their health and also in their well-being. Inequalities, it seems, extend far beyond the school gate. In Chapter 3, we turned our focus to the schools themselves. While the desire for good schools for all pupils remains evident, at least in theory, the expansion of high-stakes tests and school accountability measures (such as league tables) means that the pressure on schools to generate excellent examination outcomes is very strong. Of course, you can argue that what else are schools for if not to educate the young for a competitive and highly skilled workplace? Recent governments have invested both money and their political reputations in improving the nation's schools and, with their plans for academies and free schools, the current government is no different. That school experiences are frequently unequal is revisited in Chapter 4 that concentrates on just one outcome of schooling:

examination success. It reveals the unequal outcomes that affect many of our children, particularly those from the poorest homes. Chapter 5 was a short chapter that looked specifically at young people with special educational needs and explored two differing perspectives on the inclusion debate. As a counter to the attention which is often paid to school academic outcomes, Chapter 6 explored pupils' own perceptions of schooling and the role that schools have in helping shape socially and morally responsible citizens. Chapter 7 looked beyond compulsory schooling to consider the impact that our expanding higher education sector has had on improving social justice, particularly among groups who were traditionally less likely to participate. It reveals that despite an increase in the proportion of under-represented groups who attend HE, deep inequalities in terms of who studies what subject still remain. Firmly in 'the front line against poverty and inequality' (Cameron 2009) the nation's schools and colleges have been charged with producing a technically skilled and competent workforce capable of ensuring the country's economic competitiveness in an increasingly globalised community. From the other perspective, commentators argue that 'our obsessive focus on growth through educational engineering has had the side effect of narrowing policy thinking to the *detriment* of the least advantaged' (Wolf, 2000: 253, emphasis added). This is an important issue for policies which seek to widen participation and encourage the educationally disengaged to return to learning and was the focus of Chapter 8.

What Role for Schools?

Are we expecting too much from our schools? One thing that this book has attempted to show is that educational inequalities are not just linked to educational issues, rather that they all too often merely reflect those inequalities, be it health, crime or housing, that persist in wider society. For example, I was involved in a study several years ago for the Basic Skills Agency in which we looked at the relationship between basic attainment in Maths, Science and English and other indicators of relative disadvantage (Gorard et al. 2004). It was perhaps unsurprising to find that attainment in these subjects at every level, from Key Stage 1 through to Key Stage 5, were all related to indicators of disadvantage. Measures such as local economic activity rates, the proportion of those on benefit, social housing, health scores and rates of teenage pregnancy, which on the surface might have limited links to education, were in fact highly correlated. Of course, this was just one of many, many studies that all reach similar conclusions: that 'inequalities in initial education could be viewed as simply a manifestation of profound multiple social disadvantage' (Gorard and Smith 2007: 154).

That social and educational factors interact is, of course, not news to policymakers either. In their proposals for the reform of post-16 education and training, the previous government were quite clear that 'the factors that affect young people's participation between the ages of 16 and 24 often have their roots much earlier in their life' (DCSF 2009b: 13). The White Paper *The Importance of Teaching* argues that the gap between the rich and the poor is ethically 'indefensible' (DfE 2010b: 1). And a recent report commissioned by the Social Exclusion Task Force stresses the need to 'break the intergenerational cycle of deprivation by increasing support for poor families with children in order to improve the life chances of the next generation' (Social Exclusion Task Force 2009: 4). More recently, the Deputy Prime Minister Nick Clegg unveiled the Coalition government's Strategy for Social Mobility, the aim of which is to make social mobility the 'principal goal' of their social policy (Cabinet Office 2011: 11) and whose mission appears at the very start of this book.

Being Upwardly Mobile?

Like fairness, social mobility is another big word-of-the-moment, a piece of 'coalition candy', in the view of one commentator (Jenkins 2011). To be socially mobile suggests that an individual has moved further up the social ladder in comparison to their parents (OECD 2010d). In a relatively immobile society an individual's education level, occupation or income is very similar to that of their parents. In a more mobile society these factors would be comparatively higher: for example, an individual may have gained a university degree while their parents left school at 16. Whether social mobility is getting better or worse in Britain is a contentious topic (see, for example, Blanden et al. 2005; Gorard 2008; Crawford et al. 2011).

Let us take just one example. One piece of evidence used by those who argue that social mobility has become worse is the fact that 62 per cent of the current British government's Cabinet were privately educated; this is twice as high as the Cabinets under Labour (Sutton Trust 2010a). Similarly in the 2010 Parliament over a third of MPs had attended independent schools, of whom 20 had been educated at Eton (Sutton Trust 2010b; see also Sutton Trust 2010c and remember that only about 7 per cent of the British population are educated in the independent sector). This apparent stalling of social mobility has been a particularly potent topic among sections of the media (for example, Cohen 2005), several of whom have attributed the phenomenon to the decline of the grammar schools (see Boliver and Swift 2011). The argument they present is that the grammar school system which selected by ability (and therefore allowed the bright children of the poor to access a 'quality' education) had been replaced by comprehensive schools and an expanding selective system which selected according to wealth and so enhanced the educational divide between the rich and the poor. The consequences of this, we are told, are apparent several decades later in the composition of our most distinguished professions. However, recent research demonstrates that the move away from grammar schools towards a comprehensive system of schooling has had no impact on social mobility and that 'comprehensive schools were as good for mobility as the selective schools they replaced' (Boliver and Swift 2011: 89). Yet another example of the complex educational problems we need to be able to tackle.

So What Can be Done to Reduce Educational Inequalities?

For such an apparently difficult question it is interesting that there are often so many ready political answers. Both Iain Duncan Smith (the former leader of the Conservative Party and Founder of the Centre for Social Justice) and Frank Field (a former Labour MP) emphasise the importance of early interventions, the centrality of the family and initiatives such as parenting skills embedded in the school curriculum (Allen and Duncan Smith 2008, Field 2010).

In their recent report on intergenerational social mobility the OECD suggests that educational policies *can* make a difference in improving social mobility. They argue that higher enrolment in early childhood education programmes reduces the link between a child and their parent's academic achievement. However, they contrast this with school practices which group children into different curricula at early ages and which do not encourage a good mix of pupils from different backgrounds (OECD 2010d). Consider the recent policy proposals that we have examined in this book (for example, Sure Start and free schools). Do you think that proposals such as this will be the policies that the OECD says are needed to promote social mobility?

This is not to say that early childhood interventions and other policies aimed at educational issues are not important. However, for some commentators the answer lies not with education at all, but rather with matters that are much more fundamental. For example, Wilkinson and Pickett, the authors of *The Spirit Level* that we looked at in Chapter 2, offer a very different perspective. For them, social equality depends on greater income equality, that is in reducing the gap between the highest and lowest earners, while the economist Will Hutton calls for the state to act to ensure fairness and for a 'new culture and a new spirit … in which public action, responsive engagement and a commitment to fairness combine with the genius of capitalist markets and firms to drive us forward' (2010: 394).

Hopefully this book has helped you understand some of the main educational inequalities which persist in Britain today. It should also have shown you how many of these inequalities are not just educational issues but relate to wider society as well. So what is to be done? It is easy to become disheartened. But it is important to remember that the attainment of young people in school continues to rise, that most of those in school consider their experiences to be fair and also that it *is* possible to reduce the numbers of children who live in poverty. Labour succeeded in doing this to some extent, although perhaps by not enough.

As to the future, the very fact that terms such as fairness, justice, inequality and social mobility are now central to current political discourse and have seeped into public consciousness is, of course, a good thing. We might be quicker now to hold politicians accountable for their promises to make society fairer and less unjust. However, the success of any of their policies at a time of recession, of deepening spending cuts and of a changing relationship between the state and the people will, of course, remain to be seen.

Final Thoughts

What can schools do to prevent 'poor children from becoming poor adults'? Below are two comments about the relationship between education and social characteristics:

According to Brighouse and Swift (2010: 8):

> Nobody should expect school reforms to have huge effects on student achievement. Children spend most of their waking hours outside school, and the educational experiences and opportunities they enjoy in their families and communities vary greatly, in ways that track their social-class background reasonably closely.

In his recent independent review of poverty and life chances Frank Field concluded that:

> It is family background, parental education, good parenting and the opportunities for learning and development in those crucial years that together matter more to children than money in determining whether their potential is realised in adult life. (2010: 5)

Would you agree with these statements? What do they say about efforts to improve schools and the educational chances of children and young people?

Given all that we have read about the seemingly intractable nature of many educational and social inequalities, we do need to ask the question: 'are all inequalities bad?'. Margaret Thatcher would likely answer that inequalities are not necessarily a bad thing. Rather being unequal (or the chance of being unequal) can motivate people to do better and perhaps to succeed.

What are your views on this?

References

Abrams, F. (2010) *Learning to Fail: How Society Lets Young People Down*. London: Routledge.

Adonis, A. (2008) 'Academies and Social Mobility'. Speech to the National Academies Conference, London, 7 February, accessed from: http://webarchive.nationalarchives. gov.uk/tna/+/http://www.dcsf.gov.uk/speeches/speech.cfm?SpeechID=749.

Agassi, A. (2009) *Open: An Autobiography*. New York: HarperCollins.

Ainley, P. and Allen, M. (2010) *Lost Generation? New Strategies for Youth and Education*. London: Continuum.

Ainscow, M., Booth, T. and Dyson, A. with Farrell, P., Frankham, J., Gallannaugh, F., Howes, A. and Smith, R. (2006) *Improving Schools, Developing Inclusion*. London: Routledge.

Allen, R. (2010) 'Replicating Swedish "free school" reforms in England', *Research in Public Policy*, Summer, accessed from: http://www.bris.ac.uk/cmpo/publications/bulletin/sum-mer10/swedishfreeschools.pdf.

Archer, L., Hutchings, M. and Ross, A. (2003) *Higher Education and Social Class: Issues of Exclusion and Inclusion*. London: RoutledgeFalmer.

Arora, B. (2010) 'Citizenship education and black and minority ethnic communities', in J. Arthur and I. Davies (eds), *The Routledge Education Studies Textbook*. London: Routledge.

Artiles, A., Murri, N. and Rostenberg, D. (2006) 'Inclusion as social justice', *Theory into Practice*, 45 (3): 260–8.

Attwood, R. (2010) 'Mind the gap', *Times Higher Education Supplement*, 26 February, accessed from: http://www.timeshighereducation.co.uk/story.asp?sectioncode=26&storycode=410531&c=2.

Bailey, R., Barrow, R., Carr, D. and McCarthy, C. (eds) (2010) *The Sage Handbook of Philosophy of Education*. London: Sage.

Ball, S. (2007) *Education Plc: Understanding Private Sector Participation in Public Sector Education*. London: Routledge.

Ball, S. J. (ed.) (2004) *The RoutledgeFalmer Reader in Sociology of Education*. London: RoutledgeFalmer.

Barber, M. (1995) 'The school that had to die', *Times Educational Supplement*, 17 November, accessed from: http://www.tes.co.uk/article.aspx?storycode=13031.

Baty, P. (2003) 'Bristol "proud" of state pupil surge', *Times Higher Education Supplement*, 28 February, accessed from: http://www.timeshighereducation.co.uk/story.asp?storyCode=175041&sectioncode=26.

BBC (2002) '"No free lunch" students told', *BBC News Online*, accessed from: http://news.bbc.co.uk/1/hi/education/2479919.stm.

BBC (2003) '"Irresponsible" Hodge under fire', *BBC News Online*, accessed from: http://news.bbc.co.uk/1/hi/education/2655127.stm.

BBC (2005) 'First-time buyers on poverty "knife-edge"', *BBC News Online*, accessed from: http://news.bbc.co.uk/2/hi/business/4081596.stm.

BBC (2006) 'Teachers "bullied by online grading"', *BBC News Online*, accessed from: http://news.bbc.co.uk/1/hi/uk/6139626.stm.

BBC (2008) 'The curse of the meddling parent', *BBC News Online*, accessed from: http://news.bbc.co.uk/1/hi/7169429.stm.

BBC (2010a) 'Rich–poor divide "wider than 40 years ago"', *BBC News Online*, accessed from: http://news.bbc.co.uk/1/hi/8481534.stm.

BBC (2010b) 'Welfare spending to be cut by £4bn, says George Osborne', *BBC News Online*, accessed from: http://www.bbc.co.uk/news/uk-politics-11250639.

BBC (2010c) 'The deserving or undeserving poor?' *BBC News Online*, accessed from: http://www.bbc.co.uk/news/magazine-11778284.

BBC (2010d) 'Road risk higher among deprived children, says study', *BBC News Online*, accessed from: http://www.bbc.co.uk/news/uk-10989119.

BBC (2010e) 'Early intervention grant is cut by 11%', *BBC News Online*, accessed from: http://www.bbc.co.uk/news/education-11990256.

BBC (2010f) '209,000 university hopefuls miss out on degree places', *BBC News Online*, 16 November, accessed from: http://www.bbc.co.uk/news/education-11765127.

BBC (2010g) 'Uni fees subsidy for Welsh students', *BBC News Online*, 30 November, accessed from: http://www.bbc.co.uk/news/uk-wales-11889053.

BBC (2010h) 'Tuition fee vote day as it happened', *BBC News Online*, accessed from: http://news.bbc.co.uk/2/hi/uk_news/9275169.stm.

BBC (2011a) 'Many children's centres "under threat of closure"', *BBC News Online*, accessed from: http://www.bbc.co.uk/news/education-12182994.

BBC (2011b) 'Number of school academies triples to more than 600', *BBC News Online*, accessed from: http://www.bbc.co.uk/news/education-12998461.

BBC (2011c) 'Tuition fees: "most universities" want to charge £9,000', *BBC News Online*, accessed from: http://www.bbc.co.uk/news/education-13116975.

Beauchamp College (2010) Insted Programme, accessed from: http://www.beauchamp.leics.sch.uk/page.php?article=675&name=insted.

Bibbings, L. S. (2006) 'Widening participation and higher education', *Journal of Law and Society*, 33 (1): 74–91.

Birkett, D. (2011) 'The school I'd like: are pupils' dreams being realised?', *The Guardian*, 25 January, accessed from: http://www.guardian.co.uk/education/2011/jan/25/the-school-i-would-like.

BIS (2010a) 'Student finance', Department for Business, Innovation and Skills, accessed from: http://www.bis.gov.uk/news/topstories/2010/Nov/student-finance.

BIS (2010b) 'The Spending Review 2010', Department for Business, Innovation and Skills, 20 October, accessed from: http://www.bis.gov.uk/news/topstories/2010/Oct/BIS-CSR.

BIS (2010c) 'Progressive plans for higher education', Department for Business, Innovation and Skills, 3 November, accessed from: http://nds.coi.gov.uk/content/Detail.aspx?ReleaseID=416343&NewsAreaID=2.

BIS (2010d) *Securing a Sustainable Future for Higher Education: An Independent Review of Higher Education Funding and Student Finance* (The Browne Review), Department for Business Innovation and Skills, accessed from: http://www.bis.gov.uk/assets/biscore/corporate/docs/s/10-1208-securing-sustainable-higher-education-browne-report.pdf.

Blair, A. (2005) 'Poorer students still miss out at elite universities', *The Times*, 15 December.

Blair, T. (1997) '21 Steps to 21st Century Education – Blair'. Speech at the University of Birmingham, accessed from: http://www.prnewswire.co.uk/cgi/news/release?id=40765.

Blair, T. (1998) *The Third Way: The Renewal of Social Democracy*. Bristol: Polity Press.

Blanden, J. and Machin, S. (2004) 'Educational inequality and the expansion of UK higher education', *Scottish Journal of Political Economy*, 51 (2): 230–49.

Blanden, J., Gregg, P. and Machin, S. (2005) *Intergenerational Mobility in Europe and North America*, report supported by the Sutton Trust, Centre for Economic Performance, London School of Economics, accessed from: http://cep.lse.ac.uk/about/news/IntergenerationalMobility.pdf.

Boliver, V. (2011) 'Expansion, differentiation and the persistence of social class inequalities in British higher education', *Higher Education*, 61: 229–4.

Boliver, V. and Swift, A. (2011) 'Do comprehensive schools reduce social mobility?' *British Journal of Sociology*, 62 (1): 89–110.

Bourdieu, P. (1977) 'Cultural reproduction and social reproduction', in J. Karabel and A. H. Halsey (eds), *Power and Ideology in Education*. New York: Oxford University Press.

Bousted, M. (2010) 'For flexibility and freedoms, read "chaos"', *Times Education Supplement*, 18 June.

Bradshaw, J. (2009) 'Social inclusion and child poverty', in *Changing Childhood in a Changing Europe*. Strasbourg: European Science Foundation, pp. 29–36.

Bradshaw, J. and Richardson, D. (2009) 'An index of child well-being in Europe', *Child Indicators Research*, 2 (3): 319–51.

Branigan, T. (2002) 'Top school's creationists preach value of biblical story over evolution', *The Guardian*, 9 March, accessed from: http://www.guardian.co.uk/uk/2002/mar/09/schools.religion.

Brighouse, H. (2006) *On Education*. Abingdon: Routledge.

Brighouse, H. and Swift, A. (2008) 'Putting educational equality in its place', *Education Finance and Policy*, 3 (4): 444–66.

Broecke, S. and Hamed, J. (2008) *Gender Gaps in Higher Education Participation: An Analysis of the Relationship between Prior Attainment and Young Participation by Gender, Socio-Economic Class and Ethnicity*, DIUS Research Report 08 14, accessed February 2010 from: http://www.dius.gov.uk/research_and_analysis/~/media/publications/D/DIUS_RR_08_14.

Brown, G. (2005) *The Hugo Young Memorial Lecture*, Chatham House, 13 December, accessed from: http://www.guardian.co.uk/politics/2005/dec/13/labour.uk.

Brown, G. (2007) Speech at the University of Greenwich, 31 October, accessed from: http://webarchive.nationalarchives.gov.uk/+/http://www.number10.gov.uk/Page13675.

Brown, G. (2010) 'Gordon Brown "This election will be about social mobility"'. Speech given to the Fabian Society New Year conference, January, accessed from: http://www.publicservice.co.uk/feature_story.asp?id=13530.

Brown, M. (1998) 'The tyranny of the international horse race', in R. Slee, G. Weiner and S. Tomlinson (eds), *School Effectiveness for Whom? Challenges to the School Effectiveness and School Improvement Movements*. London: Falmer Press.

Burke, C. and Grosvenor, I. D. (2003) *The School I'd Like*. London: Routledge.

Burke, E. (1790) 'Reflections on the Revolution in France', *Great Literature Online: 1997–2011*, accessed from: http://burke.classicauthors.net/ReflectionsOnTheRevolutionInFrance/ReflectionsOnTheRevolutionInFrance4.html.

Butler, P. (2011) 'Sure Start cuts mark the end of the children's centre dream', *The Guardian*, 13 May, accessed from: http://www.guardian.co.uk/global/patrick-butler-cuts-blog/2011/may/13/haringey-cuts-to-sure-start-centres?CMP=twt_gu.

Bynner, J. (1992) *ESRC 16–19 Initiative: The Route to Careers and Identities*, ESRC 16–19 Initiative Occasional Paper 43. London: City University.

Bynner, J. and Parsons, S. (2002) 'Social exclusion and the transition from school to work: the case of young people not in education, employment, or training (NEET)', *Journal of Vocational Behaviour*, 60 (2): 289–309.

Bynner, J., Ferri, E. and Shepherd, P. (1997) *Twenty-Something in the 1990s: Getting On, Getting By, Getting Nowhere*. Aldershot: Ashgate.

Cabinet Office (2009) *Unleashing Aspiration: The Final Report of the Panel on Fair Access to the Professions*, accessed from: http://news.bbc.co.uk/1/shared/bsp/hi/pdfs/21_07_09_fair_access.pdf.

Cabinet Office (2011) *Opening Doors, Breaking Barriers: A Strategy for Social Mobility*, Cabinet Office, April, accessed from: http://download.cabinetoffice.gov.uk/social-mobility/opening-doors-breaking-barriers.pdf.

Callender, C. and Jackson, J. (2008) 'Does the fear of debt constrain choice of university and subject of study?' *Studies in Higher Education*, 33 (4): 405–29.

Cameron, D. (2007) *Social Responsibility: The Big Idea for Britain's Future*. London: Conservative Party.

Cameron, D. (2009) 'The Big Society'. Speech, 10 November, accessed from: http://www.conservatives.com/News/Speeches/2009/11/David_Cameron_The_Big_Society.aspx.

Cameron, D. (2010a) Speech to the Conservative Party conference, Birmingham, October, accessed from: http://www.guardian.co.uk/politics/2010/oct/06/david-cameron-speech-tory-conference.

Cameron, D. (2010b) 'Building the Big Society'. Speech to mark launch of Big Society programme, 18 May, accessed from: http://www.number10.gov.uk/news/topstorynews/2010/05/big-society-50248.

Campbell, T. (2010) *Justice: Issues in Political Theory*. Basingstoke: Palgrave Macmillan.

Canning, D. and Bowser, D. (2010) 'Investing in health to improve the wellbeing of the disadvantaged: reversing the argument of *Fair Society, Healthy Lives* (The Marmot Review)', *Social Science and Medicine*, 71: 1223–6.

Centre for Research on Education Outcomes (2009) *Multiple Choice: Charter School Performance in 16 States*. Stanford, CA: CREDO.

Centre for Social Justice (2009) *Early Intervention: Good Parents, Great Kids, Better Citizens*, 2nd edn, Centre for Social Justice and Smith Institute, accessed from: http://www.centrefo:rsocialjustice.org.uk/client/downloads/CSJ%20Early%20Intervention%20paper%20WEB%20(2).pdf.

Chevalier, A. and Lindley, J. (2009) 'Overeducation and the skills of UK graduates', *Journal of the Royal Statistical Society: Series A (Statistics in Society)*, 172 (2): 307–37.

Children's Commissioner for Wales (2011) 'What We Do', accessed from: http://www.childcom.org.uk/en/what-do-we-do/.

Chilosi, D., Noble, M., Broadhead, P. and Wilkinson, M. (2010) 'Measuring the effect of Aimhigher on schooling attainment and higher education applications and entries', *Journal of Further and Higher Education*, 34 (1): 1–10.

Chowdry, H., Crawford, C., Dearden, L., Goodman, A. and Vignoles, A. (2010) *Widening Participation in Higher Education: Analysis Using Linked Administrative Data*. London: IFS/ESRC, accessed from: http://www.ifs.org.uk/wps/wp1004.pdf.

Chua, A. (2011) *Battle Hymn of the Tiger Mother*. New York: Bloomsbury.

Cigman, R. (2010) 'Let's not get too social and emotional about learning', *Questa*, Issue 1: 'Could Do Better? Education Policies in an Election Year', March.

Civic Education Study (2001) 'IEA Civic Education Study', accessed from: http://www2. huberlin.de/empir_bf/iea_e.html.

Coe, R. (2009) 'School improvement: reality and illusion', *British Journal of Educational Studies*, 57 (4): 363–79.

Coffield, F. (1998) 'A tale of three little pigs: building the learning society with straw', *Evaluation and Research in Education*, 12 (1): 44–58.

Cohen, M. (1998) '"A habit of healthy idleness": boys' underachievement in historical perspective', in D. Epstein, J. Elwood, V. Hey and J. Maw (eds), *Failing Boys? Issues in Gender and Achievement*. Buckingham: Open University Press.

Cohen, N. (2005) 'Long live grammars', *The Observer*, Sunday, 31 July.

Coldron, J., Cripps, C. and Shipton, L. (2010) 'Why are English secondary schools socially segregated?' *Journal of Education Policy*, 25 (1): 19–35.

Coleman, J., Campbell, E., Hobson, C., McPartland, J., Mood, A., Weinfeld, F. and York, R. (1966) *Equality of Educational Opportunity*. Washington, DC: US Government Printing Office.

Coles, B., Godfrey, C., Keung, A., Parrott, S. and Bradshaw, J. (2010) 'Estimating the lifetime Cost of NEET: 16–18 Year Olds Not in Education, Employment or Training'. Research undertaken for the Audit Commission, University of York, accessed from: http://www.york.ac.uk/depts/spsw/research/neet/NEET_Final_Report_July_2010_York.pdf.

Committee on Higher Education (1963) *Higher Education*, Report of the Committee appointed by the Prime Minister under the Chairmanship of Lord Robbins (The Robbins Report). London: HMSO.

Condron, D. J. (2011) 'Egalitarianism and educational excellence: compatible goals for affluent societies?' *Educational Researcher*, 40 (2): 47–55.

Connell, R. W. (1994) 'Cool guys, swots and wimps: the interplay of masculinity and education', *Oxford Review of Education*, 15 (3): 291–303.

Connor, H., Burton, R., Pearson, R., Pollard, E. and Regan, J. (1999) *Making the Right Choice: How Students Choose Universities and Colleges*. London: Universities UK.

Cooke, G. and Lawton, K. (2008) *Working Out of Poverty: A Study of the Low Paid and the 'Working Poor'*. London: Institute for Public Policy Research.

Cooke, R., Barkham, M., Audin, K., Bradley, M. and Davy, J. (2004) 'How social class differences affect students' experience of university', *Journal of Further and Higher Education*, 28 (4): 407–21.

Crawford, C., Johnson, P., Machin, S. and Vignoles, A. (2011) 'Social Mobility: A Literature Review', Department for Business, Innovation and Skills, accessed from: http://www.bis.gov.uk/assets/biscore/economics-and-statistics/docs/s/11-750-social-mobility-literature-review.pdf.

Croft, J. (2011) *Profit-Making Free Schools Unlocking the Potential of England's Proprietorial Schools Sector*, Adam Smith Research Trust, accessed from: http://www.adamsmith.org/files/ASI_School_report_WEB.pdf.

Croll, P. (2009) 'Educational participation post-16: a longitudinal analysis of intentions and outcomes', *British Journal of Educational Studies*, 57 (4): 400–16.

Curtis, A., Exley, S., Sasia, A., Tough, S. and Whitty, J. (2008) *The Academies Programme: Progress, Problems and Possibilities*, a report for the Sutton Trust, accessed from: http://www.suttontrust.com/research/the-academies-programme-progress-problems-and-possibilities/.

Cusworth, L., Bradshaw, J., Coles, B., Keung, A. and Chzhen, Y. (2009) *Understanding the Risks of Social Exclusion Across the Life Course: Youth and Young Adulthood*, A Research Report for the Social Exclusion Task Force. London: Cabinet Office.

Dale, R. (2000) 'Thinking ahead, commentary: what the "Third Way" is really about', *New York Times*, 4 April, accessed from: http://www.nytimes.com/2000/04/04/business/worldbusiness/04iht-think.2.t.html.

Darling-Hammond, L. (2007) 'Race, inequality and educational accountability: the irony of "No Child Left Behind"', *Race, Ethnicity and Education*, 10 (3): 245–60.

Data Service (2009) 'LFS Regional and Sub-regional Estimates of Education Attainment', accessed from: http://www.thedataservice.org.uk/statistics/statisticalfirstrelease/sfr_supplementary_tables/labour_force_survey_sfr_supplementary_tables/.

Daugherty, R. (2009) 'National curriculum assessment in Wales: adaptations and divergence', *Educational Research*, 51 (2): 247–50.

Davies, P., Mangan, J. and Hughes, A. (2009) 'Participation, financial support and the marginal student', *Higher Education*, 58 (2): 193–204.

Davison, J. (2010) 'Education and social class', in J. Arthur and I. Davies (eds), *The Routledge Education Studies Textbook*. London: Routledge.

DCSF (2007) *Raising Expectations: Staying in Education and Training Post-16*. Nottingham: DCSF Publications.

DCSF (2008) *Attainment by Pupil Characteristics, in England 2007/08*, accessed from: http://www.education.gov.uk/rsgateway/DB/SFR/s000822/index.shtml.

DCSF (2009a) *Gender and Education: Gapbusters – Schools That Close or Narrow the Attainment Gap Between Boys and Girls in English*. London: DCSF.

DCSF (2009b) *Investing in Potential: Our Strategy to Increase the Proportion of 16–24 Year Olds in Education, Employment or Training*. London: DCSF.

Dearden, L., Emmerson, C., Frayne, C. and Meghir, C. (2009) 'Conditional cash transfers and school dropout rates', *Journal of Human Resources*, 44 (4): 827–57.

DEFRA (2009) *Sustainable Development Indicators in Your Pocket 2009: An Update of the UK Government Strategy Indicators*. London: Department for Environment, Food and Rural Affairs, accessed October 2010 from: http://www.defra.gov.uk/sustainable/government/progress/documents/SDIYP2009_a9.pdf.

Delamont, S. (1999) 'Gender and the discourse of derision', *Research Papers in Education*, 14 (1): 3–21.

Denham, J. (2008) 'Widening Participation'. Speech to the Higher Education Funding Council Conference, 8 April, in Warwick, UK, accessed from: http://www.dius.gov.uk/speeches/denham_HEFCE_080408.html.

Department for Innovation, Universities and Skills (2009) *The Demand for Science, Technology, Engineering and Mathematics (STEM) Skills*, accessed March 2010 from: http://www.bis.gov.uk/assets/biscore/corporate/migratedd/publications/d/demand_for_stem_skills.pdf.

Department for Work and Pensions (2010) *Households Below Average Income Statistics First Release*, accessed from: http://statistics.dwp.gov.uk/asd/hbai/hbai_2009/pdf_files/first_release_0809.pdf.

Department of Health (2010) *Health Profile of England, 2009,* accessed from: http://www.dh.gov.uk/publications.

Department of Trade and Industry (1998) *Our Competitive Future: Building the Knowledge Driven Economy*, White Paper, December. London: Stationery Office.

DES (1965) *The Organisation of Secondary Education*, Circular 10/65. London: HMSO.

DfE (2010a) *Early Intervention Grant – FAQs*, accessed from: http://www.education.gov.uk/childrenandyoungpeople/earlylearningandchildcare/a0070357/early-intervention-grant-frequently-asked-questions/.

DfE (2010b) *The Importance of Teaching*, The Schools White Paper 2010, accessed from: http://www.education.gov.uk/publications/eOrderingDownload/CM-7980.pdf.

DfE (2010c) *Academy Model Extended So Every School Can Benefit*, Department for Education Press Notice, 17 November 2011, accessed from: http://www.education.gov.uk/schools/leadership/typesofschools/academies/whatisanacademy/a0068006/academy-model-extended-so-every-school-can-benefit.

DfE (2010d) *142 Schools to Convert to Academy Status Weeks After Academies Act Passed*, Department for Education Press Notice, 1 September 2010, accessed from: http://www.education.gov.uk/inthenews/pressnotices/a0064203/142-schools-to-convert-to-academy-status-weeks-after-academies-act-passed.

DfE (2010e) Letter from Secretary of State about the Free School Programme, accessed from: media.education.gov.uk/assets/files/pdf/l/letter%20from%20the%20secretary%20of%20state%20to%20las%20introducing% 20free%20schools.pdf.

DfE (2010f) *Special Educational Needs in England, January 2010*, Statistical First Release, accessed from: http://www.education.gov.uk/rsgateway/DB/SFR/s000939/sfr19-2010.pdf.

DfE (2010g) *The Importance of Teaching*, White Paper Equalities Impact Assessment, accessed from: https://www.education.gov.uk/publications/eOrderingDownload/CM-7980-Impact_equalities.pdf.

DfE (2010h) *NEET Statistics – Quarterly Brief*, November, accessed from: http://www.education.gov.uk/rsgateway/DB/STR/d000969/Quarterly-Brief-NEET-Q32010_final.pdf.

DfE (2011a) *Sure Start Children's Centres Statutory Guidance*, accessed from: http://www.education.gov.uk/childrenandyoungpeople/earlylearningandchildcare/surestart/a0074514/sure-start-childrens-centres-statutory-guidance.

DfE (2011b) *Open Academies Map and Schools Submitting Applications*, accessed from: http://www.education.gov.uk/schools/leadership/typesofschools/academies/a0069811/schools-submitting-applications-and-academies-which-have-opened-in-201011.

DfE (2011c) *Free School Proposals*, accessed from: http://www.education.gov.uk/schools/leadership/typesofschools/freeschools/b0066077/approved-free-school-proposals/.

DfE (2011d) *School Spending Data*, accessed from: http://www.education.gov.uk/schools/adminandfinance/financialmanagement/b0072409/background/.

DfE (2011e) *Support and Aspiration: A New Approach to Special Educational Needs and Disability: A Consultation.* London: Stationery Office.

DfE (2011f) *Review of the National Curriculum in England: Remit,* accessed from: http://www.education.gov.uk/schools/teachingandlearning/curriculum/nationalcurriculum/b0073043/remit-for-review-of-the-national-curriculum-in-england/.

DfE (2011g) *Plans to End the Education Maintenance Allowance (EMA) Programme,* accessed from: http://www.education.gov.uk/inthenews/a0073028/plans-to-end-the-education-maintenance-allowance-ema-programme.

DfEE (1997) *Excellence for All Children: Meeting Special Educational Needs.* London: HMSO.

DfES (2000) *Youth Cohort Study: Education, Training and Employment of 16–18 Year Olds in England and the Factors Associated with Non-participation,* Statistical Bulletin Number 02/2000, accessed from: http://www.education.gov.uk/rsgateway/DB/SBU/b000162/b02-2000.pdf.

DfES (2001) *Schools Building on Success: Raising Standards, Promoting Diversity, Achieving Results,* Cm 5050. London: HMSO, accessed from: http://www.archive.official-documents.co.uk/document/cm50/5050/5050.pdf.

DfES (2002) *Citizenship: The National Curriculum for England,* accessed from: http://www.dfes.gov.uk/citizenship.

DfES (2003a) *Every Child Matters: Change for Children.* London: TSO.

DfES (2003b) *Widening Participation in Higher Education.* London: DfES.

DfES (2006) *Widening Participation in Higher Education.* London: DfES, accessed from: http://www.dcsf.gov.uk/hegateway/uploads/6820-DfES-WideningParticipation2.pdf.

DfES (2007) *Gender and Education:* The Evidence on Pupils in England. London: DfES.

Docking J. (1996) *National School Policy. Major Issues in Education Policy for Schools in England and Wales, 1979 Onwards.* London: David Fulton.

Dore, R. (1997) *The Diploma Disease,* 2nd edn. London: Institute of Education, University of London.

Dorling, D. (2010) *Inequality.* Bristol: Policy Press.

Dyson, A. (2001) 'Special needs in the twenty-first century: where we've been and where we're going', *British Journal of Special Education,* 28 (1): 24–9.

Ecclestone, K. and Hayes, D. (2008) *The Dangerous Rise of Therapeutic Education.* London: Routledge.

Education Week (2003) 'Admissions case could have impact on K-12 education', *Education Week,* 11 December.

Epstein, D., Elwood, J., Hey, V. and Maw J. (1998) *Failing Boys? Issues in Gender and Achievement.* Buckingham: Open University Press.

Equalities Review (2007) *Fairness and Freedom: The Final Report of the Equalities Review,* accessed from: http://www.communities.gov.uk/publications/corporate/fairnessfreedom.

Equality and Human Rights Commission (2010) *How Fair is Britain?,* accessed from: http://www.equalityhumanrights.com/key-projects/how-fair-is-britain/.

Ertl, H. (2006) 'Educational standards and the changing discourse on education: the reception and consequences of the PISA Study in Germany', *Oxford Review of Education,* 32 (5): 619–34.

European Social Protection Committee (2008) *Child Poverty and Well-Being in the EU Current Status and Way Forward*, European Commission, accessed from: http://www.libertysecurity.org/IMG/pdf_ke3008251_en.pdf.

Eurostat (2010a) *Unemployment Rate by Age Group (Under 25)*, accessed from: http://epp.eurostat.ec.europa.eu/tgm/table.do?tab=table&init=1&language=en&pcode=tsdec460&plugin=1.

Eurostat (2010b) *Young People Not in Employment and Not in Any Education and Training*, data accessed February 2011 from: http://epp.eurostat.ec.europa.eu/portal/page/portal/product_details/dataset?p_product_code=EDAT_LFSE_20.

Feinstein, L. (2003) *How Early Can We Predict Future Education Achievement*, LSE Centre Piece, Summer, accessed from: http://cep.lse.ac.uk/centrepiece/v08i2/feinstein.pdf.

Feinstein, L., Duckworth, K. and Sabates, R. (2008) *Education and the Family: Passing Success Across the Generations*. London: Routledge.

Ferguson, D. (2008) 'International trends in inclusive education: the continuing challenge to teach each one and everyone', *European Journal of Special Needs Education*, 23 (2): 109–20.

Field, F. (2010) *The Foundation Years: Preventing Poor Children Becoming Poor Adults*, Report of the Independent Review on Poverty and Life Chances, accessed from: http://webarchive.nationalarchives.gov.uk/20110120090128/http://povertyreview.independent.gov.uk.

Fisher, T. (2010) 'The death of meritocracy: exams and university admissions in crisis', *Forum*, 52 (2): 213–32.

Fitz, J., Davies, B. and Evans, J. (2006) *Educational Policy and Social Reproduction: Class Inscription and Symbolic Culture*. Abingdon: Routledge.

Flatley, J., Kershaw, C., Smith, K., Chaplin, R. and Moon, D. (2010) *Crime in England and Wales 2009/10*, Findings from the British Crime Survey and Police Recorded Crime, July 2010, 12/10. London: Home Office, accessed October 2010 from: http://rds.home office.gov.uk/rds/pdfs10/hosb1210.pdf.

Fletcher, M. (2009) *Should We End the Education Maintenance Allowance?*, CfBT Educational Trust, accessed from: http://www.cfbt.com/evidenceforeducation/pdf/1.EMA_v4(FINAL)W.pdf.

Forsyth, A. and Furlong, A. (2000) *Socioeconomic Disadvantage and Access to Higher Education*. Bristol: Policy Press.

Forsyth, A. and Furlong, A. (2003) *Losing Out? Socioeconomic Disadvantage and Experience in Further and Higher Education*. Bristol: Policy Press.

Francis, B. (2000) *Boys and Girls Achievement: Addressing the Classroom Issues*. Abingdon: RoutledgeFalmer.

Francis, B. and Skelton, C. (2005) *Reassessing Gender and Achievement: Questioning Contemporary Key Debates*. Abingdon: Routledge.

Frankenberg, E., Siegel-Hawley, G. and Wang, J. (2010) *Choice without Equity: Charter School Segregation and the Need for Civil Rights Standards*. Los Angeles: Civil Rights Project/Proyecto Derechos Civiles at UCLA, accessed from: http://www.civilrightsproject.ucla.edu.

Frean, A. and Sugden, J. (2008) 'School place lottery growing across Britain', *The Times*, 20 September, accessed from: http://www.timesonline.co.uk/tol/news/uk/education/article4791082.ece.

Frederick, K. (2005) 'Let's take the special out of special needs', *Times Educational Supplement*, 15 July, accessed from: http://www.tes.co.uk/article.aspx?storycode=2116799.

Freedman, L. (2010) 'Do academy schools really work?' *Prospect* magazine, 168, accessed from: http://www.prospectmagazine.co.uk/2010/02/in-a-league-of-their-own/.

Furedi, F. (2009) 'Intensive parenting', *Society Today*, September.

Furlong, A. (2006) 'Not a very NEET solution: representing problematic labour market transitions among early school-leavers', *Work Employment Society*, 20 (3): 553–69.

Furlong, A. and Cartmel, F. (2009) *Higher Education and Social Justice*. Buckingham: Open University Press.

Galindo-Rueda, F., Marcenaro-Gutierrez, O. and Vignoles, A. (2004) 'The widening socio-economic gap in higher education', *National Institute Economic Review*, 190 (1): 75–88.

Garner, R., Ferdinand, P. and Lawson, S. (2009) *Introduction to Politics*. Oxford: Oxford University Press.

Genda, Y. (2007) 'Jobless youths and the NEET problem in Japan', *Social Science Japan Journal*, 10 (1): 23–40.

Gillard, D. (2007) *Education in England: A Brief History*, accessed from: http://www.educationengland.org.uk/history.

Gillborn, D. (1990) *'Race', Ethnicity and Education: Teaching and Learning in Multi-ethnic Schools*. London: Unwin Hyman.

Gillborn, D. (2008) *Racism and Education Coincidence or Conspiracy?* London: Routledge.

Gillborn, D. and Youdell, D. (2000) *Rationing Education – Policy, Practice, Reform and Equity*. Buckingham: Open University Press.

Goodman, A., Sibieta, L. and Washbrook, E. (2009) *Inequalities in Educational Outcomes Among Children Aged 3 to 16*, Final Report for the National Equality Panel, accessed from: http://www.equalities.gov.uk/pdf/Inequalities%20in%20education%20outcomes%20among%20children.pdf.

Gorard, S. (2000) *Education and Social Justice*. Cardiff: University of Wales Press.

Gorard, S. (2005) 'Academies as the "future of schooling": is this an evidence-based policy?' *Journal of Education Policy*, 20 (3): 369–77.

Gorard, S. (2008) 'Research impact is not always a good thing: a re-consideration of rates of "social mobility" in Britain', *British Journal of Sociology of Education*, 29 (3): 317–24.

Gorard, S. (2009) 'What are Academies the answer to?', *Journal of Education Policy*, 24 (1): 1–13.

Gorard, S. (2010) 'Serious doubts about school effectiveness', *British Educational Research Journal*, 36 (5): 745–66.

Gorard, S. (2011) 'The potential determinants of young people's sense of justice: an international study', *British Journal of Sociology of Education*, 32 (1): 35–52.

Gorard, S. and Fitz, J. (2006) 'What counts as evidence in the school choice debate?' *British Educational Research Journal*, 32 (6): 797–816.

Gorard, S. and Rees, G. (2002) *Creating a Learning Society?* Bristol: Policy Press.

Gorard, S. and Smith, E. (2007) 'Do barriers get in the way? A review of the determinants of post-16 participation', *Research in Post-Compulsory Education*, 12 (2): 141–58.

Gorard, S. and Smith, E. (2010) *Equity in Education: An International Perspective*. Basingstoke: Palgrave Macmillan.

Gorard, S., Lewis, J. and Smith, E. (2004) 'Disengagement in Wales: educational, social and economic issues', *Welsh Journal of Education*, 13 (1): 118–47.

Gorard, S., Rees, G. and Selwyn, N. (2002) 'The "conveyor belt effect": a re-assessment of the impact of National Targets for Lifelong Learning', *Oxford Review of Education*, 28 (1): 75–89.

Gorard, S., Taylor, C. and Fitz, J. (2003) *Schools, Markets and Choice Policies*. London: RoutledgeFalmer.

Gorard, S., Adnett, N., May, H., Slack, K., Smith, E. and Thomas, L. (2007) *Overcoming the Barriers to Higher Education*. Stoke-on-Trent: Trentham Books.

Grek, S. (2008) *PISA in the British Media: Leaning Tower or Robust Testing Tool?* CES Briefing 45, April, accessed from: http://www.ces.ed.ac.uk/PDF%20Files/Brief045.pdf.

Guardian (2001a) 'The School We'd Like', *The Guardian*, 5 June, accessed from: http://www.guardian.co.uk/education/2001/jun/05/schools.uk7.

Guardian (2001b) 'Towards a National Debate'. Speech by Prime Minister James Callaghan, Ruskin College, Oxford, 18 October, reproduced in *The Guardian*, 15 October 2001, accessed from: http://education.guardian.co.uk/thegreatdebate/story/0,,574645,00.html.

Guardian (2003a) 'Taking the mick', *The Guardian*, 15th January 2003, accessed from: http://www.guardian.co.uk/politics/2003/jan/15/education.highereducation.

Guardian (2003b) 'Bristol attacks admissions "fallacy"', *The Guardian*, 4 March.

Guardian (2007) 'Ban cyber-bullying clips, Johnson to urge websites', *The Guardian*, 10 April, accessed from: http://www.guardian.co.uk/education/2007/apr/10/schools.uk2.

Guardian (2010a) 'General election 2010: surge in voter registration makes election outcome more volatile [online]', *The Guardian*, 22 April, accessed from: http://www.guardian.co.uk/politics/2010/apr/22/surge-voter-registration-election-volatile.

Guardian (2010b) 'How many privately-educated students attend each university?' *The Guardian*, 22 December, accessed from: http://www.guardian.co.uk/news/ datablog/2010/dec/22/oxbridgeandelitism-oxforduniversity#data.

Guardian (2011a) 'The school I'd like', *The Guardian*, accessed from: http://www.guardian.co.uk/education/series/the-school-i-would-like.

Guardian (2011b) 'Oxbridge elitism: how many black and poor students go to Oxford and Cambridge?' *The Guardian*, 13 April, accessed from: http://www.guardian.co.uk/news/datablog/2010/dec/07/oxbridge-elitism-oxford-cambridge-race-class.

Ha, B., McInerney, C., Tobin, S. and Torres, R. (2010) *Youth Employment in Crisis*, International Institute for Labour Studies Discussion Paper, accessed from: http://www.ilo.org/public/english/bureau/inst/download/dp201.pdf.

Hankinson, A. (2010) 'How graduates are picking up the tab for their parents' lives', *The Guardian*, 31 January, accessed from: http://www.guardian.co.uk/money/2010/jan/31/unemployed-graduates-credit-crunch-andrew-hankinson.

Hansard (2010a) Parlimentary Questions, House of Commons, 3 November, accessed from: http://www.publications.parliament.uk/pa/cm201011/cmhansrd/cm101103/debtext/101103-0001.htm.

Hansard (2010b) Commons Debates: Government Policy (NEETs), 9 November, accessed from: http://www.publications.parliament.uk/pa/cm201011/cmhansrd/cm101109/halltext/101109h0002.htm.

Hansard (2011) 'Business, Innovation and Skills: Aimhigher Programme', response to questions in the House of Commons, 24 March, accessed from: http://www.publications.parliament.uk/pa/cm201011/cmhansrd/cm110324/text/110324w0004.htm.

Hansen, K., Joshi, H. and Dex, S. (eds) (2010) *Children of the 21st Century: The First Five Years*. Bristol: Policy Press.

Harber, C. (2009) *Toxic Schooling: How Schools Became Worse?* Nottingham: Educational Heretics Press.

Health and Social Care Information Centre (2009) 'National Child Measurement Programme: England, 2008/09 School Year', National Health Service, accessed from: http://www.ic.nhs.uk/webfiles/publications/ncmp/ncmp0809/NCMP_England_2008_09_school_year_report_2.pdf.

HEFCE (2010) *Trends in Young Participation in Higher Education: Core Results for England*. Bristol: HEFCE 2010/03, accessed from: http://www.hefce.ac.uk/pubs/hefce/2010/10_03/10_03.pdf.

HESA (2010) 'All Students by Level, Mode and Domicile', accessed from: http://www.hesa.ac.uk/dox/pressOffice/sfr142/SFR142_Table1.pdf.

Hills, J. and Stewart, K. (eds) (2005) *A More Equal Society? New Labour, Poverty, Inequality and Exclusion*. Bristol: Policy Press.

Hills, J., Sefton, T. and Stewart, K. (eds) (2009) *Towards a More Equal Society? Poverty, Inequality and Policy Since 1997*. Bristol: Policy Press.

Hirsch, D. (2007) *Experiences of Poverty and Educational Disadvantage: Research Round-up*. York: Joseph Rowntree Foundation, accessed from: http://www.donaldhirsch.com/edroundup.pdf.

Hirsch, D. (2009) *Ending Child Poverty in a Changing Economy*. York: Joseph Rowntree Foundation, accessed from: http://www.jrf.org.uk.

Hobbs, G. and Vignoles, A. (2010) 'Is children's free school meal "eligibility" a good proxy for family income?' *British Educational Research Journal*, 36 (4): 673–90.

Hodkinson, A. and Vickerman, P. (2009) *Key Issues in Special Educational Needs and Inclusion*. London: Sage.

Home Office (1998) *Supporting Families*: A Consultation Document. London: TSO.

House of Commons Education and Skills Committee (2006) *Special Educational Needs*, Third Report of Session 2005–06, Volume I. London: Stationery Office.

House of Commons Education and Skills Committee (2007) *Citizenship Education*, Second Report of Session 2006–07. London: Stationery Office.

Humphrey, N., Lendrum, A. and Wigelsworth, M. (2010) *Social and Emotional Aspects of Learning (SEAL) Programme in Secondary Schools: National Evaluation*, Department for Education, Research Report DFE-RR049.

Hutton, W. (2010) *Them and Us. Changing Britain – Why We Need a Fair Society*. London: Little, Brown.

Illich, I. (1971) *Deschooling Society*. New York: Harper & Row.

ILO (2010) *Global Employment Trends for Youth*, accessed from: http://www.ilo.org/wcmsp5/groups/public/---ed_emp/---emp_elm/--- trends/documents/publication/wcms_143349.pdf.

Japan Times (2009) 'NEETS on the rise', *Japan Times*, 19 July, accessed from: http://www.lexisnexis.com.ezproxy1.lib.asu.edu/hottopics/lnacademic/?shr=t&csi=169018&sr=HLEAD(NEETs+on+the+rise)+and+date+is+2009.

Jencks, C. (1972) *Inequality: A Reassessment of the Effect of Family and Schooling in America.* New York: Basic Books.

Jenkins, S. (2011) 'Social immobility is built into the way Britain lives and learns', *The Guardian*, 5 April, accessed from: http://www.guardian.co.uk/commentisfree/2011/apr/05/social-immobility-nick-clegg-internships.

Jotangia, D., Moody, A., Stamatakis, E. and Wardle, H. (2006) *Obesity Among Children Under 11.* Department of Health.

Keating, A., Kerr, D., Benton, T., Mundy, E. and Lopes, J. (2010) *Citizenship Education in England 2001–2010: Young People's Practices and Prospects for the Future*, Eighth and Final Report from the Citizenship Education Longitudinal Study (CELS). London: Department for Education.

Kenway, P. and Palmer, G. (2007) *Poverty Among Ethnic Groups: How and Why Does It Differ?* York: Joseph Rowntree Foundation.

Kiernan, K. E. and Mensah, F. K. (2009) 'Poverty, maternal depression, family status and children's cognitive and behavioural development in early childhood: a longitudinal study', *Journal of Social Policy*, 38 (4): 569–88.

Kiernan, K. E. and Mensah, F. K. (2011) 'Poverty, family resources and children's early educational attainment: the mediating role of parenting', *British Educational Research Journal*, 37 (2): 317–36.

Knowles, G. (2009) *Ensuring Every Child Matters.* London: Sage.

Korkodilos, M. (2007) *Health Inequalities Glossary*, Expert Group on Social Determinants and Health Inequalities, European Commission Public Health and Risk Assessment Directorate.

Kozol, J. (1991) *Savage Inequalities.* New York: Harper Perennial.

Kozol, J. (2005) *The Shame of the Nation.* New York: Three Rivers Press.

Lamb Inquiry (2009) *Special Educational Needs and Parental Confidence.* Nottingham: DCSF.

Laureau, A. (1987) 'Social class differences in family–school relationships: the importance of cultural capital', *Sociology of Education*, 60: 73–85.

Lee, J. (2002) 'Racial and ethnic achievement gap trends: reversing the progress toward equity?' *Educational Researcher*, 31 (1): 3–12.

Leitch Review of Skills (2006) *Prosperity for All in the Global Economy – World-Class Skills*, Final Report, December, accessed from: http://www.ukces.org.uk/upload/pdf/2006-12%20 LeitchReview1_2.pdf.

Leo, E., Galloway, D. and Hearne, P. (2010) *Academies and Educational Reform: Governance, Leadership and Strategy.* Bristol: Multilingual Matters.

Levin, H. M. (2009) 'The economic payoff to investing in educational justice', *Educational Researcher*, 38 (1): 5–20.

Levitas, R. (1996) 'Fiddling while Britain burns? The "measurement" of unemployment', in R. Levitas, and W. Guy (eds), *Interpreting Official Statistics.* London: Routledge.

Lewis, A., Parsons, S. and Robertson, C. (2006) *My School, My Family, My Life: Telling It Like It Is.* Stratford-upon-Avon: Disability Rights Commission.

LSN (2009) *Tackling the NEETs Problem: Supporting Local Authorities in Reducing Young People Not in Employment, Education and Training.* London: Learning and Skills Network, accessed from: http://www.ioe.ac.uk/TacklingNEETs.pdf.

Lupton, R. and Power, A. (2005) 'Disadvantaged by where you live? New Labour and neighbourhood renewal', in J. Hills and K. Stewart (eds), *A More Equal Society? New Labour, Poverty, Inequality and Exclusion*. Bristol: Policy Press.

Luscombe, B. (2011) 'Chinese vs Western mothers: Q&A with Amy Chua', *Time*, 11 January, accessed from: http://healthland.time.com/2011/01/11/chinese-vs-western-mothers-q-a-with-amy-chua/.

Mac an Ghaill, M. (1988) *Young, Gifted and Black*. Buckingham: Open University Press.

MacBeath, J., Galton, M., Steward, S., MacBeath, A. and Page, C. (2006) *The Costs of Inclusion*, Report commissioned by the National Union of Teachers concerning inclusion in schools, accessed from: http://www.educ.cam.ac.uk/people/staff/galton/Costs_of_Inclusion_Final.pdf.

McCaig, C., Stevens, A. and Bowers-Brown, T. (2006) 'Does Aimhigher work? Evidence from the national evaluation', Higher Education Research Network, Sheffield, pp. 1–16, accessed from: http://shura.shu.ac.uk/2382/1/Does_Aimhigher_work_CM_AS_TB_2007.pdf.

MacLeod, D. (2008) 'In they swoop to direct their children's career: the helicopter parents have landed', *The Guardian*, 3 January, accessed from: http://www.guardian.co.uk/uk/2008/jan/03/students.highereducation.

Macnaughton, A. (2008) 'Helicopter parents: hovering – but not helping', *Sunday Times*, 13 April, accessed from: http://www.timesonline.co.uk/tol/life_and_style/education/article3734696.ece.

Maddern, K. (2010) 'Statements of intent on road to SEN revolution', *Times Educational Supplement*, 17 December, accessed from: http://www.tes.co.uk/article.aspx?storycode=6066186.

Magadi, M. and Middleton, S. (2007) *Severe Child Poverty in the UK*. London: Save the Children UK.

Maguire, S. and Thompson, J. (2007) 'Young People Not in Education, Employment or Training (NEET) – Where Is Government Policy Taking Us Now?' University of Warwick, accessed from: http://wrap.warwick.ac.uk/446/2/WRAP_Maguire_YOUTH_POLICY_FINAL_1st_June.pdf.

Mahony, P. (1998) 'Girls will be girls and boys will be first', in D. Epstein, J. Elwood, V. Hey and J. Maw (eds), *Failing Boys? Issues in Gender and Achievement*. Buckingham: Open University Press.

Mangan, J., Hughes, A., Davies, P. and Slack, K. (2010) 'Fair access, achievement and geography: explaining the association between social class and students' choice of university', *Studies in Higher Education*, 35 (3): 335–50.

Marmot Review (2010) *Fair Society, Healthy Lives: The Marmot Review Executive Summary*, accessed from: http://www.ucl.ac.uk/marmotreview.

Merrell, C. and Tymms, P. (2010) 'Changes in children's cognitive development at the start of school in England 2001–2008', *Oxford Review of Education*, first published 7 December (iFirst).

Meuret, D. (2002) 'School equity as a matter of justice', in W. Hutmacher, D. Cochrane and N. Bottani (eds), *In Pursuit of Equity in Education*. Dordrecht: Kluwer Academic.

Millar, F. and Young, T. (2010) 'The debate: should parents set up schools?' *Times Educational Supplement*, 29 January, accessed from: http://www.tes.co.uk/article.aspx?storycode=6034470.

Millard, E. (1997) 'Differently literate: gender identity and the construction of the developing reader', *Gender and Education*, 9 (1): 31–48.

Miller, D. (2003) *Political Philosophy: A Very Short Introduction.* Oxford: Oxford University
Press.

Mortimore, P. (1991) 'The nature and findings of school effectiveness research in the primary sector', in S. Riddell and S. Brown (eds), *School Effectiveness Research: Its Messages
for School Improvement.* London: HMSO.

Mortimore, P., Sammons, P., Stoll, L., Lewis, D. and Ecob, R. (1988) *School Matters: The
Junior Years.* Wells: Open Books.

Mullis, I. V. S., Martin, M. O., Kennedy, A. M. and Foy, P. (2007) *PIRLS 2006 International
Report*, Boston College, TIMSS & PIRLS International Study Center, accessed from: http://
pirls.bc.edu/PDF/P06_IR_FrontMatter.pdf.

Murphy Paul, A. (2011) 'Tiger moms: is tough parenting really the answer?' *Time*, 20
January, accessed from: http://www.time.com/time/nation/article/0,8599,2043313-2,00.
html.

Murray, J. (2010) 'Students hit by scrapping of education maintenance allowance', *The
Guardian*, 25 October, accessed from: http://www.guardian.co.uk/education/2010/
oct/25/education-maintenance-allowance.

NAO (2002) *Widening Participation in Higher Education in England.* London: Stationery Office.

NAO (2008) *Widening Participation in Higher Education.* London: Stationery Office, accessed
February 2010 from: http://www.nao.org.uk/publications/0708/widening_participa-
tion_in_high.aspx.

NAO (2010) *The Academies Programme.* London: Stationery Office, accessed from: http://
www.nao.org.uk/publications/1011/academies.aspx.

National Academy of Sciences (2007) *Rising Above the Gathering Storm: Energizing and
Employing America for a Brighter Economic Future*, accessed November 2009 from: http://
books.nap.edu/openbook.php?record_id=11463&page=86.

National Equality Panel (2010) *An Anatomy of Economic Inequality in the UK*, Report of the
National Equality Panel, January 2010. London: Government Equalities Office, accessed
October 2010 from: http://www.equalities.gov.uk/pdf/NEP%20Report%20bookmarked-
final.pdf.

NCEE (1983) *A Nation at Risk?* Accessed from: http://www.njafter3.org/edu/docs/
Reports_A-Nation-At-Risk.pdf.

NCES (2009) *NAEP 2008: Trends in Academic Progress*, National Center for Education Statistics,
accessed from: http://nces.ed.gov/nationsreportcard/pdf/main2008/2009479.pdf.

NCES (2011) 'College Navigator: Arizona State University', accessed from: http://nces.
ed.gov/collegenavigator/?s=AZ&ct=1&id=104151#expenses.

NCIHE (1997) *Higher Education in the Learning Society*, The Dearing Report, National
Committee of Inquiry into Higher Education, accessed from: https://bei.leeds.ac.uk/
Partners/NCIHE/.

Neill, A. S. (1964) *Summerhill: A Radical Approach to Education.* London: Victor Gollancz.

NESS (2005) *Early Impacts of Sure Start Local Programmes on Children and Families: Report of
the Cross-sectional Study of 9- and 36-Month Old Children and Their Families*, National
Evaluation of Sure Start Research Report NESS/2005/FR/01, accessed from: http://www.
education.gov.uk/publications/eOrderingDownload/NESS-2005-FR-013.pdf.

NESS (2008) *The Impact of Sure Start Local Programmes on Three Year Olds and Their Families,* National Evaluation of Sure Start Research Report NESS/2008/FR/027. London: DfES.

NESS (2010) *The Impact of Sure Start Local Programmes on Five Year Olds and Their Families,* National Evaluation of Sure Start Research Brief DFE-RB067, accessed from: http://www.ness.bbk.ac.uk/impact/documents/RB067.pdf.

Nevada Department of Education (2010) *Nevada Department of Education: AYP results by county 2009–2010,* accessed from: http://www.doe.nv.gov/AYP_Results_County.htm.

Newton, P. E. (2005) 'The public understanding of measurement inaccuracy', *British Educational Research Journal,* 31 (4): 419–42.

OECD (2001) *Knowledge and Skills for Life: First Results from PISA 2000.* Paris: OECD.

OECD (2003) *Beyond Rhetoric: Adult Learning Policies and Practices.* Paris: OECD.

OECD (2008) *Growing Unequal? Income Distribution and Poverty in OECD Countries.* Paris: OECD, accessed from: http://www.oecd.org/els/social/inequality/GU.

OECD (2009) Doing Better for Children. Paris: OECD, accessed from: http://www.oecd.org/els/social/childwellbeing.

OECD (2010a) *Country Statistical Profiles 2010: United Kingdom,* accessed from: http://stats.oecd.org/index.aspx?queryid=23111.

OECD (2010b) *PISA 2009 Results: What Students Know and Can Do: Student Performance in Reading, Mathematics and Science,* Vol. I. Paris: OECD.

OECD (2010c) *PISA 2009 Results: Overcoming Social Background Equity in Learning Opportunities and Outcomes,* Vol. II. Paris: OECD.

OECD (2010d) 'A family affair: intergenerational social mobility across OECD countries', in *Economic Policy Reforms: Going for Growth 2010.* Paris: OECD, chapter 5, accessed from: http://www.oecd.org/document/51/0,3343,en_2649_34117_44566259_1_1_1_1,00.html.

OECD (2010e) *Education at a Glance.* Paris: OECD.

OECD (2011a) 'Household income', in *Society at a Glance 2011.* Paris: OECD.

OECD (2011b) *OECD Economic Surveys: United Kingdom,* March 2011, accessed from: http://www.spectator.co.uk/article_assets/articledir_13578/6789298/OECD%20Economic%20Survey%20of%20the%20UK.pdf.

Ofsted (1999) Summerhill Inspection Report, accessed from http://www.ofsted.gov.uk/oxedu_reports/download/(id)/70512/(as)/124870_106164.pdf.

Ofsted (2007) Summerhill Inspection Report, accessed from: http://www.ofsted.gov.uk/oxedu_reports/download/(id)/90088/(as)/124870_301621.pdf.

Ofsted (2010) *The Special Educational Needs and Disability Review: A Statement Is Not Enough,* accessed from: http://www.osfted.gov.uk.

OHCHR (2006) *Convention on the Rights of Persons with Disabilities,* accessed from: http://www2.ohchr.org/english/law/disabilities-convention.htm.

ONS (2009) *Family Spending: A Report on the 2008 Living Costs and Food Survey.* Basingstoke: Palgrave Macmillan, accessed October 2010 from: http://www.statistics.gov.uk/downloads/theme_social/Family-Spending-2008/FamilySpending2009.pdf.

ONS (2010a) 'Social Trends Spotlight on e-Society', *Social Trends,* 1 (1): 1–12, accessed from: http://www.statistics.gov.uk/articles/social_trends/socialtrends-spotlight-on-e-society.pdf.

ONS (2010b) *Labour Force Survey, Summary Aged 16 to 59/64,* accessed from: http://www.statistics.gov.uk/statbase/product.asp?vlnk=15384.

ONS (2010c) *Internet Access 2010, Households and Individuals*, Office for National Statistics Statistical Bulletin, accessed from: http://www.statistics.gov.uk/pdfdir/iahi0810.pdf.

ONS (2011) *Neighbourhood Statistics*, accessed from: http://www.neighbourhood.statistics. gov.uk/dissemination/.

Orfield, G. (2000) 'Policy and equity: lessons of a third of a century of educational reforms in the United States', in F. Reimers (ed.), *Unequal Schools, Unequal Chances: The Challenges to Equal Opportunity in the Americas*. Cambridge, MA: Harvard University Press.

Osler, A. (2010) *Students' Perspectives on Schooling*. Maidenhead: Open University Press.

Passy, R. and Morris, M. (2010) *Evaluation of Aimhigher: Learner Attainment and Progression*, Final Report, NFER, accessed from: http://www.hefce.ac.uk/pubs/rdreports/2010/ rd15_10/rd15_10.pdf.

Phillips, R. (2003) 'Education policy, comprehensive schooling and devolution in the disUnited Kingdom: an historical "home international" analysis', *Journal of Education Policy*, 18 (1): 1–17.

Pickett, K. and Dorling, D. (2010) 'Against the organization of misery? The Marmot Review of health inequalities', *Social Science and Medicine*, 71: 1231–3.

Platt, L. (2011) *Understanding Inequalities: Stratification and Difference*. Cambridge: Polity Press.

Potton, E. (2010) 'Young People in the Labour Market: Key Issues for the New Parliament', House of Commons Library Research, accessed January 2011 from: http://www.parlia-ment.uk/documents/commons/lib/research/key%20issues/Key%20Issues%20 Young%20people%20in%20the%20labour%20market.pdf.

Poverty Site (2010a) *Income Inequalities*, accessed from: http://www.poverty.org.uk/09/ index.shtml#note1.

Poverty Site (2010b) *Numbers in Low Income*, accessed from: http://www.poverty.org. uk/01/index.shtml.

Poverty Site (2010c) *Lacking in Essentials*, accessed from: http://www.poverty.org.uk/10/ index.shtml#num.

Poverty Site (2010d) *Low Income and Ethnicity*, accessed from: http://www.poverty.org. uk/06/index.shtml?2.

Prais, S. (2003) 'Cautions on OECD's recent educational survey (PISA)', *Oxford Review of Education*, 29 (2): 139–63.

Prince's Trust (2010a) *The Cost of Exclusion: Counting the Cost of Youth Disadvantage in the UK*. London: Prince's Trust.

Prince's Trust (2010b) *The Prince's Trust YouGov Youth Index 2010*. London: Prince's Trust.

Prince's Trust (2011) *The Prince's Trust Macquarie Youth Index*. London: Prince's Trust, accessed from: http://www.princes-trust.org.uk/pdf/Youth_Index_jan2011.pdf.

Pring, R. (2010) 'The philosophy of education and educational practice', in R. Bailey, R. Barrow, D. Carr and C. McCarthy (eds), *The Sage Handbook of Philosophy of Education*. London: Sage.

Pyke, N. (1997) 'Education is social justice, says Blair', *Times Educational Supplement*, 18 April, accessed from: http://www.tes.co.uk/article.aspx?storycode=46786.

QCA (1998) *Education for Citizenship and the Teaching of Democracy in Schools*, Final Report of the Advisory Group on Citizenship (The Crick Report). London: QCA.

Raffe, D. (2003) *Young People Not in Education, Employment or Training*, University of Edinburgh, Centre for Educational Sociology, accessed from: http://www.ces.ed.ac.uk/PDF%20Files/Brief029.pdf.

Raffe, D., Croxford, L., Iannelli, C., Shapira, M. and Howieson, C. (2006) *Social-Class Inequalities in Education in England and Scotland*, Special CES Briefing No. 40, May, Centre for Educational Sociology, accessed February 2010 from: http://www.ces.ed.ac.uk/PDF%20Files/Brief040.pdf.

Rafferty, M. (1970) *Summerhill: For and Against*. New York: Hart.

Raffo, C., Dyson, A., Gunter, H., Hall, D., Jones, L. and Kalambouka, A. (2007) *Education and Poverty: A Critical Review of Theory, Policy and Practice*, Joseph Rowntree Foundation, accessed from: http://www.jrf.org.uk/sites/files/jrf/2028-education-poverty-theory.pdf.

Randall, J. (2010) 'A-level results: how the great university boom has defrauded our students', *Daily Telegraph*, 19 August.

Raphael Reed, L. (1998) '"Zero tolerance": gender performance and school failure', in D. Epstein, J. Elwood, V. Hey and J. Maw (eds), *Failing Boys? Issues in Gender and Achievement*. Buckingham: Open University Press.

Rawls, J. (2001) *Justice as Fairness: A Restatement*. Cambridge, MA: Harvard University Press.

Reay, D. (2006) '"I'm not seen as one of the clever children": consulting primary school pupils about the social conditions of learning', *Educational Review*, 58 (2): 171–81.

Reay, D. and Ball, S. (1998) '"Making their minds up": family dynamics of school choice', *British Educational Research Journal*, 24 (4): 431–48.

Reay, D., David, M. and Ball, S. (2005) *Degrees of Choice: Social Class, Race, Gender in Higher Education*. Stoke-on-Trent: Trentham Books.

Rees, G., Goswami, H. and Bradshaw, J. (2010) *Developing an Index of Children's Subjective Well-Being in England*, Report for the Children's Society, accessed from: http://www.childrenssociety.org.uk.

Rees, G., Williamson, H. and Istance, D. (1996) '"Status zerO": a study of jobless school-leavers in South Wales', *Research Papers in Education*, 11 (2): 219–35.

Rose, R. and Shevlin, M. (2004) 'Encouraging voices: listening to young people who have been marginalised', *Support for Learning*, 19 (4): 155–61.

Ruitenberg, C. and Vokey, D. (2010) 'Equality and justice', in R. Bailey, R. Barrow, D. Carr and C. McCarthy (eds), *The Sage Handbook of Philosophy of Education*. London: Sage.

Rutter, M., Maughan, B., Mortimore, P. and Ouston, J. (1979) *Fifteen Thousand Hours: Secondary Schools and Their Effects on Children*. London: Open Books.

St Clair, R., Tett, L. and Maclachlan, K. (2010) *Scottish Survey of Adult Literacies, 2009: Report of Findings*. Glasgow: Scottish Government Social Research, accessed from: http://www.scotland.gov.uk/Resource/Doc/319174/0102005.pdf.

Sammons, P. (2007) *School Effectiveness and Equity: Making Connections. A Review of School Effectiveness and Improvement Research – Its Implications for Practitioners and Policy Makers*. Reading: CfBT Education Trust, accessed from: http://www.cfbt.com/evidenceforeducation/pdf/Full%20Literature%20Review.pdf.

Sammons, P., Hillman, J. and Mortimore, P. (1995) *Key Characteristics of Effective Schools – A Review of School Effectiveness Research*. London: Ofsted.

Sandel, M. J. (2010) *Justice: What's the Right Thing to Do?* London: Penguin.

Saporito, S. and Sahoni, D. (2006) 'Mapping educational inequality: concentrations of poverty among poor and minority students in public schools', *Social Forces*, 85: 1227–53.

Saunders, P. (2010) *Beware False Prophets: Equality, the Good Society and the Spirit Level*. London: Policy Exchange, accessed from: http://www.policyexchange.org.uk/images/publications/pdfs/Beware_False_Prophets_Jul_10.pdf.

Selwyn, N. (2011) *Education and Technology: Key Issues and Debates*. London: Continuum.

Selwyn, N., Gorard, S. and Furlong, J. (2005) *Adult Learning in the Digital Age*. London: Routledge.

Shepherd, J. (2009) 'Bristol v Bolton: opposite ends of the prosperity ladder', *The Guardian*, 3 February.

Sibieta, L., Chowdry, H. and Muriel, A. (2008) *Level Playing Field? The Implications of School Funding*, Centre for British Teachers Research Report, accessed from: http://www.ifs.org.uk/docs/level_playing.pdf.

Simmons, R. (2010) 'Raising the age of compulsory education in England: a NEET solution?' *British Journal of Educational Studies*, 56 (4): 420–39.

Simola, H. (2005) 'The Finnish miracle of PISA: historical and sociological remarks on teaching and teacher education', *Comparative Education*, 41 (4): 455–70.

Skelton, C., Carrington, B., Francis, B., Hutchings, M., Read, B. and Hall, I. (2009a) 'Gender "matters" in the primary classroom: pupils' and teachers' perspectives', *British Educational Research Journal*, 35 (2).

Skelton, C., Francis, B. and Moss, G. (2009b) *Gender and Education – Mythbusters*. Nottingham: DCSF Publications, accessed from: http://www.education.gov.uk/publications/standard/SchoolsSO/Page11/DCSF-00599-2009.

Slavin, R. E. (2002) 'Evidence-based education policies: transforming educational practice and research', *Educational Researcher*, 31 (7): 15–21.

Slee, R. (2011) *The Irregular School: Exclusion, Schooling and Inclusive Education*. London: Routledge.

Smith, E. (2003) 'Failing boys and moral panics: perspectives on the underachievement debate', *British Journal of Educational Studies*, 51 (3): 282–95.

Smith, E. (2005a) 'Raising standards in American schools: the case of No Child Left Behind', *Journal of Educational Policy*, 20 (4): 507–24.

Smith, E. (2005b) *Analysing Underachievement in Schools*. London: Continuum.

Smith, E. (2010a) 'Underachievement, failing boys and moral panics', *Evaluation and Research in Education*, 23 (1): 37–49.

Smith, E. (2010b) 'Do we need more scientists? A long-term view of patterns of participation in UK Undergraduate Science Programmes', *Cambridge Journal of Education*, 40 (3): 281–98.

Smith, E. (2012) 'Women into science and engineering? Gendered patterns of participation in UK STEM subjects', *British Educational Research Journal*, in press.

Smith, E. and Gorard, S. (2006) 'Pupils' views of equity in schools', *Compare*, 36 (1): 41–56.

Smith, E. and White, P. (2011) 'Who is studying science? The impact of widening participation policies on the social composition of UK undergraduate science programmes', *Journal of Education Policy*, in press.

Smith, M. P., Olatunde, O. and White, C. (2010) 'Monitoring inequalities in health expectancies in England – small area analyses from the Census 2001 and General Household

Survey 2001–05', *Health Statistics Quarterly*, No. 46, Summer 2010. Newport: Office for National Statistics, accessed August 2010 from: http://www.statistics.gov.uk/hsq/downloads/hsq46.pdf.

Smithers, R. (2003) 'Private schools boycott Bristol over selection', *The Guardian*, Wednesday, 5 March.

Smyth, E. and McCoy, S. (2009) *Investing in Education: Combating Educational Disadvantage*, Report for Barnardos, Research Series Number 6. Dublin: Economic and Social Research Institute.

Social Exclusion Task Force (2009) *Understanding the Risks of Social Exclusion Across the Life Course*: Youth and Young Adulthood. London: Cabinet Office.

Social Exclusion Unit (1999) *Bridging the Gap: New Opportunities for 16–18 Year Olds Not in Education, Employment or Training*, Cm 4405. London: Stationery Office.

Spielhofer, T., Golden, S., Evans, K., Marshall, H., Mundy, E., Pomati, M. and Styles, B. (2010) *Barriers to Participation in Education and Training*, Research Report DFE-RR009, accessed from: http://www.education.gov.uk/publications/eOrderingDownload/DFE-RR009.pdf.

Spring, J. (2011) *American Education*, 14th edn. McGraw-Hill.

Stevenson, J. and Lang, M. (2010) 'Social class and higher education: a synthesis of research', EvidenceNet, Higher Education Academy, accessed from: http://www.heacademy.ac.uk/evidencenet.

Stewart, K. and Hills, J. (2005) 'Introduction', in J. Hills and K. Stewart (eds), *A More Equal Society? New Labour, Poverty, Inequality and Exclusion*. Bristol: Policy Press.

Stewart, W. (2008) 'Pupil voice to become law', *Times Educational Supplement*, 14 November, accessed from: http://www.tes.co.uk/article.aspx?storycode=6005072.

Storey, P. and Chamberlin, R. (2001) *Improving the Take Up of Free School Meals*, DfEE Research Report RR270. London: Department for Education and Employment.

Strand, S. (2011) 'The limits of social class in explaining ethnic gaps in educational attainment', *British Educational Research Journal*, 37 (2): 197–229.

Sunderman, G. (2008) *Holding NCLB Accountable: Achieving Accountability, Equity and School Reform*. New York: Corwin Press.

Sutton Trust (2010a) *The Educational Backgrounds of Government Ministers in 2010*, Report for the Sutton Trust, accessed from: www.suttontrust.com/research/?&p=2.

Sutton Trust (2010b) *The Educational Backgrounds of Members of Parliament in 2010*, Report for the Sutton Trust, accessed from: http://www.suttontrust.com/research/?&p=2.

Sutton Trust (2010c) *Educational Mobility in England: The Link Between the Educational Levels of Parents and the Educational Outcomes of Teenagers*, Report for the Sutton Trust, accessed from: http://www.suttontrust.com/research/?&p=2.

Swift, A. and Brighouse, H. (2010) 'School choice for those who have no choice', *Questa*, Issue 1: 'Could Do Better? Education Policies in an Election Year', March.

Tawney, R. H. (1922) *Secondary Education for All: A Policy for Labour*. London: Labour Party.

Thatcher, M. (1975) 'Let Our Children Grow Tall'. Speech to the Institute of SocioEconomic Studies, New York City, September, accessed from: http://www.margaretthatcher.org/document/102769.

Thatcher, M. (1985) Speech to Conservative Central Council, 23 March, accessed from: http://www.margaretthatcher.org/document/106000.

Thatcher, M. (1987) 'Society Speech', interview for *Woman's Own* Magazine, September, accessed from: http://www.margaretthatcher.org/document/106689.

Thomas, B., Dorling, D. and Smith, G. D. (2010) 'Inequalities in premature mortality in Britain: observational study from 1921 to 2007', *British Medical Journal*, 341: c3639.

Thomas, G. and Vaughan, M. (2004) *Inclusive Education: Readings and Reflections.* Maidenhead: Open University Press.

Thomas, J. (2009) *Current Measures and the Challenges of Measuring Children's Wellbeing*, Working Paper, Office for National Statistics, accessed from: http://www.statistics.gov.uk/downloads/theme_social/Measuring-childrens-wellbeing.pdf.

Thurow, L. C. (1977) 'Education and economic equality', in J. Karabel and A. H. Halsey (eds), *Power and Ideology in Education.* New York: Oxford University Press.

Tice, R. (2008) *Academies: A Model Education?* London: Reform.

Tomlinson, S. (1987) *Ethnic Minorities in British Schools: A Review of the Literature, 1960–1982.* London: Heinemann.

Torney-Purta, J., Lehmann, R., Oswald, H. and Schulz, W. (2001) *Citizenship and Education in Twenty-Eight Countries: Civic Knowledge and Engagement at Age 14.* Amsterdam: IEA.

UCAS (2010) *UCCA/PCAS/UCAS Applicants and Accepts 1962–2009: FT Undergraduate, All Domiciles*, UCAS statistical services, accessed November 2010 from: http://www.ucas.ac.uk/documents/stats/PCASUCAS62-09table.pdf.

UKCES (2009) *The Employability Challenge: Full Report*, accessed from: http://www.ukces.org.uk/upload/pdf/EmployabilityChallengeFullReport.pdf.

UNESCO (2011) *Education for All: Global Monitoring Report*, accessed from: http://www.unesco.org/new/en/education/themes/leading-the-international-agenda/efareport/.

UNICEF (2005) *Child Poverty in Rich Countries 2005*, Innocenti Report Card No. 6, accessed from: http://www.unicef-irc.org/publications/pdf/repcard6e.pdf.

UNICEF (2007) *Child Poverty in Perspective: An Overview of Child Well-Being in Rich Countries*, UNICEF Innocenti Research Centre, Report Card No. 7, accessed from: http://www.unicef.org/media/files/ChildPovertyReport.pdf.

UNICEF (2011) *A Summary of the United Nations Convention on the Rights of the Child*, accessed from: http://www.unicef.org.uk/Documents/Publication-pdfs/crcsummary.pdf?epslanguage=en.

University of Michigan (2003) *Admissions Lawsuits: Factsheets*, accessed from: http://www.vpcomm.umich.edu/admissions/faqs/facts.html.

Vincent, C., Braun, A. and Ball, S. (2010) 'Local links, local knowledge: choosing care settings and schools', *British Educational Research Journal*, 36 (2): 279–98.

Ward, H. (2011) 'A Sure Start, but how likely is a happy ending?' *Times Educational Supplement*, 4 March, accessed from: http://www.tes.co.uk/article.aspx?storycode=6071826.

Ward, S. and Eden, C. (2009) *Key Issues in Education Policy.* London: Sage.

Warnock, M. and Norwich, B. (2010) *Special Educational Needs: A New Look*, ed. L. Terzi. London: Continuum.

Watson, S. (2006) *A Global Guide to Management Education*, Global Foundation for Management Education, accessed November 2010 from: http://www.gfme.org/global_guide/pdf/263-268%20UK.pdf.

West, A. and Currie, P. (2008) 'The role of the private sector in publicly funded schooling in England: finance, delivery and decision making', *Policy and Politics*, 36 (2): 191–207.

West, M. and Peterson P. (2003) 'The politics and practice of school accountability', in P. Peterson and M. West (eds), *No Child Left Behind? The Politics and Practice of School Accountability*. Washington, DC: Brookings Institution.

White, P. (in press) 'Modelling the "learning divide": predicting participation in adult learning and future learning intentions 2002 to 2010', *British Educational Research Journal*, available from: http://www.tandfonline.com/doi/abs/10.1080/01411926.2010.529871.

Wilkinson, R. and Pickett, K. (2010) *The Spirit Level: Why Equality Is Better for Everyone*. London: Penguin Books.

Williamson, H. (2004) *The Milltown Boys Revisited*. Oxford: Berg.

Willis, P. (1977) *Learning to Labour: How Working Class Kids Get Working Class Jobs*. Aldershot: Gower.

Wolf, A. (2000) *Does Education Matter? Myths About Education and Economic Growth*. London: Penguin.

Wolf, A. (2008a) 'Educational expansion: the worms in the apple', *Economic Affairs*, 25 (1): 36–40.

Wolf, A. (2008b) 'Diminished Returns How Raising the Leaving Age to 18 Will Harm Young People and the Economy', Policy Exchange, accessed from: http://www.policyexchange. org.uk/images/publications/pdfs/Diminished_Returns.pdf.

Wolf, A. (2009) *An Adult Approach to Further Education*. London: Institute of Economic Affairs, accessed from: http://www.iea.org.uk/sites/default/files/publications/files/upld-book498pdf.pdf.

Wolf, A. (2011) *Review of Vocational Education* (The Wolf Report), March, Department for Education, accessed from: http://www.education.gov.uk/publications/eOrderingDownload/The%20Wolf%20Report.pdf.

Wolf, A., Jenkins, A. and Vignoles, A. (2006) 'Certifying the workforce: economic imperative or failed social policy', *Journal of Education Policy*, 21 (5): 535–65.

Wood, E. (2003) 'The power of pupil perspectives in evidence-based practice: the case of gender and underachievement', *Research Papers in Education*, 18 (4): 365–83.

Wyness, M. (2006) 'Children, young people and civic participation: regulation and local diversity', *Educational Review*, 58 (2): 209–18.

Younger, M. and Warrington, M. with Gray, J., Ruddock, J., McLellan, R., Bearne, E., Kershner, R. and Bricheno, P. (2005) *Raising Boys' Achievement*. London: DfES.

Index